Jack,

You are entering a great time in life. Looking to the future is very important now. Everything you do builds your character and habits. Habits control us, so take care how you build.

Be a huge, monsterous, charging rhino and charge for your dreams!

Matt Granger

'08

Build Yourself For Success
A Kid's Guide to Success

Written and Illustrated by

Matt Granger

Success4Kids Publishing
Wheaton, Il
Order from www.booksurge.com

ISBN 1-59109-958-7

Build Yourself For Success

Contents

Introduction

Growing up today is hard. So many things try to get your attention to tell you what to do and what to think. Your parents come to mind about now, don't they? They want to teach you what to do and what to think because they love you more than you can imagine. You can pretty much trust what your parents tell you because they wouldn't try to hurt you.

Beware. Not all of the things that try to get your attention have your best interest in mind. Take the TV and movies, for example. Many of the shows that kids watch have a dangerous message. For example, who would you say is smarter, Bart or Homer Simpson? Who is more in charge, Bart or Homer? Who is cooler, Bart or Homer? Shows like the Simpson's send a message that parents and adults are dumb, not cool, and not worthy of your respect.

Then there's the violence in movies, shows, and video games. Look at how popular Power Rangers, Pokémon, Digimon, and WWF wrestling are. They make kids less shocked by killing and fighting.

Music can also send dangerous messages. Many popular songs are about drugs or alcohol. Some musicians use them and sing about how cool they think drugs and drinking are. Some songs make gangs sound cool. Other songs are about hopelessness. The singer has no hope in his life and sings about the despair he feels. This can make people who listen to it depressed and hopeless too.

What do you have to wear to be cool? Is it a certain brand of shoe? A certain label of clothes? A particular hair style? Do you have to be in a certain group to be liked and fit in? Yes, your friends can also send wrong messages sometimes. Many times they don't mean to, but the message is sent–You aren't worth as much if you don't do the right things.

The purpose of this book is to tell you that you are worth more than you know. That is the first step to being successful. That is what your parents want you to know. We want you to build yourself for success.

Success is a lifelong journey. You choose to move toward success with each thought and action, or you choose to move away from success. The choice is yours. If you start thinking like a winner now, you'll act like a winner now.

Positive and negative messages get stuck in your mind. The negative messages will always be around. You don't have to look too hard to find them. Unfortunately, you have to search for positive messages. That's where this book can help. The purpose of this book is to start flooding your mind with good thoughts now. That will lead you to good actions and attitudes. It will help you to be more successful. It will also help to erase some of the negative messages. It is harder to do as you grow older because there are more negative messages to erase.

I know what I'm talking about. My parents got divorced when I was in first grade. My younger sister and I lived with my mom. A few years later, my dad came and kidnapped us. We lived with him from third grade on.

My dad and stepmother drank too much alcohol. They got drunk almost every day. I felt alone in the world. We didn't have a lot of money or nice things either. Everyone at school teased me because I wore K-Mart tennis shoes instead of Nike shoes. We were on welfare. That means that the government gave us money each month because my dad wasn't making enough money. The government also gave us food stamps. They are like money that can only be used for food. The kids that knew about that teased me about it.

I didn't like me, my life, or living. I even thought about ending my own life. I thought that no one, not even my dad, would miss me. The kids at school wouldn't even know I was gone, unless they noticed that the kid they teased every day wasn't there anymore. There was nothing positive in my life.

Then I met Gene Obenrader. He was my Sunday School teacher. He was interested in what was going on with me and wanted to help. He started giving me positive messages. The problem was that there were so many negative thoughts filling my head that I couldn't really believe there was anything good about me. Beware! You start to believe what you hear over and over again. It becomes real to you. It becomes you. Another way to say it is that you become the messages that you hear about yourself over and over again.

Gene told me a story that challenged me. I always used the negative messages I believed about myself as an excuse. "It's no wonder I can't do this," I would say. "Look at all the bad things I've had to deal with." The story he told made me think about that.

He told about twin boys who grew up with an alcoholic father. One boy grew up to be an alcoholic and had a lot of family problems. The other one grew up to be the president of a large company. When someone asked them why they ended up where they were in life, they gave the same answer: "What would you expect with the father I had." The one who grew up to be an alcoholic used what he went through as an excuse to fail. He saw himself as an innocent victim. It gave him permission in his own mind not to try. The other one used it as a reason. He didn't want to end up like his dad, so he did everything he could to succeed. He chose to succeed. He didn't see himself as a victim to feel sorry for. He wanted to be a winner who decided to overcome the things that happened to him.

That story started to change how I looked at myself. I started to decide not to use my past as an excuse. It was just something that I would have to overcome. I made some decisions that put my life on a path away from some of the things that were negative in my life. I made the choice not to drink alcohol, like my dad. I decided that I would never get a divorce. I decided that I would be a good dad someday. But there were so many negative messages about myself in my head that it just wasn't that simple. I had a lot of doubt to whether I could pull it off.

Seventeen years after hearing the story about the two brothers I was still struggling with the negative messages. Some of the negative thoughts still kept me from trying. I was afraid to fail. I wouldn't even get dressed up because I couldn't handle it when someone said I looked nice. I didn't feel good enough about myself to accept the compliment.

As you can see, I know how hard it is to erase the negative thoughts. Remember, they become you. It's hard to change what you believe about yourself. Then I started reading books and listening to tapes about being successful, failing correctly, and choosing which messages that you hear. I went looking for positive messages, and the changes in my thinking started to change me.

I became a teacher because I wanted to help kids. I know that there are a lot of kids that are going through some bad stuff, like I did. I wanted to give positive messages to them. For the first eleven years I feel like I did OK. I still didn't believe in myself, so it was hard to believe in others and encourage them. As I read those books and listened to those tapes, I began to collect quotes that could be positive messages to me.

I've been learning that becoming successful is a process that happens with each thought. You either listen to the negative messages or the positive messages. Each thought moves you farther along on the success journey or it makes you stop. The choice is yours.

I believe that reading this book, and many others like it, will put you so far ahead of your peers that they will never catch up. Most people get out of college and get their first job. Then they may say, "Now that I have started my career, what do I have to do to be successful?" Then they will start looking at books to learn how to be successful. You have this book in your hands now. If you read and use what's in it, you will start developing the habits, attitudes, goals, and knowledge that the rest will begin to develop when they are adults. You will have a head start, and they will never catch you.

I want to help you out on your journey. So, I decided to take the quotes I've collected and put them into a book and explain each one. The journey is so much easier if you choose to fill your mind with positive messages. I hope this book is the first step on a lifelong success journey.

Thanks God for giving my life purpose. To all the people who believed in me before I believed in myself, this is a reflection of all I learned from you. Thanks Mom and Dad. God used everything to make me into the right person in the right place at the right time to write this. And to everyone reading this, I hope this is a first step on a great adventure.

MG

Chapter 1

Success

If you are going to build yourself for success, you should know what success is. You should also understand failure, which many people think is the opposite of success. The first thing to understand is that failure and success aren't one-time things that happen. You won't be successful when you do a certain thing. It isn't a one-time event. You aren't a failure if you mess up once either.

Success is a journey, a trip, that you take. It is something that happens each time you choose to believe the positive messages over the negative messages. It is something that happens every time you choose the truth over the lies. That is what the positive and negative messages are really. The positive messages are the truth about you. The negative messages are the lies that others have told about what they think you are. Choosing the truth leads you on the path of success. Choosing the lies moves you on the path of failure. Choose carefully!

Success is growing a little each day. William J. H. Boetcker said, "Never mind what others do; do better than yourself, beat your own record from day to day, and you are a success." He means that if you just grow a little each day, if you beat your old marks, you are a success. Success isn't something that happens *to* you. It is something that happens *in* you. You are competing with yourself, not others. If you end the day a little better than you started, you grew that day. Put together a string of days like that, and you have a successful week. Put some weeks together and your month was successful. As the months pile up you have a successful year. As successful years pass you are fortunate to have had a successful life. That is the goal!

Keep growing!

❧

"The difference between the successful person and others is not a lack of strength, not a lack of knowledge, but rather a lack of will."

It takes a lot of effort to be successful. Remember that it is a daily and lifelong journey. It is putting in energy to grow and learn more each day. This quote says that there is one big difference between successful people and other people. Successful people are willing to put in the energy to succeed. They have the will to go on when it gets tough. You may have heard the saying "When the going gets tough, the tough get going." That's what this is talking about. Successful people are tough. They hang in there.

The quote also says what the difference between successful people and others isn't. It isn't that some people don't have the strength. Everyone has the strength to be successful. The power is in all of us. The seeds of greatness are in you. Real seeds need light, the right temperature, and water to start growing. Inside you is the stuff that the seeds of greatness need to start growing. But, the negative messages shut out the light and make your heart cold. It takes strength to look for positive messages to let the light in and warm your heart so the seeds can grow. When it gets too tough, many people just don't have the will to fight the negative messages.

The difference is not a lack of knowledge either. Everyone can learn something and grow each day. Knowledge is out there for anyone to use. It is in books, on the Internet, and from people who are older and can teach you things. You can learn from all of those places and many others too. It isn't just learning things in school like how lights work, the three branches of government, how to multiply, or to read better. You can also learn how to be a better person by hanging around people who are learning to be better people. You can learn how to be successful by reading books like this one. Those people who aren't successful in life don't have the will to do something positive with their time. Instead of reading a book like this, they would rather sit and watch TV for several hours. The knowledge to grow is out there for us all; successful people have the will to find it and use it.

"It's easier to go down the mountain than up, but the view is best from the top."

Have you ever been up on a mountain looking out upon the world? It is a most beautiful sight! You can see for miles and miles. If there is a town or city nearby, it looks so small and puny. It makes you think about how small the great things we build, like cities, really are. Being on the mountaintop is a great experience.

It takes a long time to drive up a mountain. The height of the mountain may be 5,280 feet, which is equal to a mile. But it would take ten to fifteen miles of roads to get up that one mile. That's because the roads have to wind back and forth. If they went straight up it would be too steep. No cars or trucks would be able to get up to the top. It takes a lot of effort to get to the top, and the road is long.

Getting down is a different story. You could shut the car off and just coast down a mountain road. It would take no energy except for the energy of gravity pulling you down. Your car wouldn't use any gas. It takes a lot less energy going down a hill.

Think about a time that you had to ride a bike up a hill. How did you feel when you got to the top? Were your legs a little tired? What happened if you stopped pedaling? Now think about riding down the same hill. Did you even have to pedal? It was a lot easier, wasn't it?

Success is like that. This quote talks about going up and down a mountain. "It is easier to go down the mountain," it says. Many people start up the mountain on a success journey, but it gets too hard. Their legs get tired of pedaling, so they stop. They think they can't make it, so they turn the bike around and coast down. They stop learning. They go to work in the morning and come home at night, day after day after day, year after year after year. When they get home they eat dinner and watch TV and collapse into bed to get up and do it all over again the next day. It is so much easier than trying to fight their way up a mountain. It doesn't mean they are bad people; they have just lost the will to fight.

Going up the mountain on the success journey is tough. I'm not going to lie and say it isn't. It is a long road, and it takes a lot of energy. Those who choose to make the journey will be rewarded. That is what the last part of the quote means. The view from the top of the mountain is better than the bottom. Becoming a better person by learning and growing each day is better than wasting time watching TV all night. As you grow you also can help others grow in their lives. That is better than just coasting through life and never making a difference to others.

The journey is tough. If it wasn't, you wouldn't enjoy the rewards as much. Let's climb the mountain together.

"Every obstacle is a stepping stone to your success."

Have you ever tried crossing a stream without stepping in the water? Maybe you had to get across a large puddle without getting your shoes soaked. How did you do it? You look for stones in the stream that are out of the water. You can step from stone to stone to get across. Maybe there are spots in the puddle that are not as deep. You use those to get across without getting soaked. Those spots or stones that you walk on are called stepping stones. They help us get to where we are going.

We all have problems. Every person has things that are hard to do. We'll call these struggles. There are things that we aren't good at. No one is good at everything. That is true for everyone. We all have fears. Some people are afraid to fail. Others are afraid of people. The problems we face, our struggles, and our fears are obstacles. Obstacles are things that get in our way.

The quote says that our problems and struggles are actually stepping-stones on our success journey. They can help us get to where we want to go. You grow as a person each time you choose not to let your problems, fears, or struggles get in your way. Every day you grow takes you farther on your success journey.

Your obstacles can be an excuse or a reason. Many people use their obstacles as an excuse to fail or do nothing. In the introduction I mentioned a man who became an alcoholic because his father was one. He used his dad as an *excuse* to fail. Do you remember his brother? He became very successful because he used his dad as a *reason* to do well. Winners use their obstacles as reasons to do well.

I like telling this to my students: "Excuses are like armpits. Everyone has them, and they all stink." Excuses and armpits stink. You will have to choose each time things get hard. Will you make an excuse to quit, or will you see it as a reason to succeed?

"On the road to success, you can be sure of one thing... there is never a crowd on the extra mile.

Two thousand years ago the Romans ruled the world. Rome is a city in Italy. But they controlled land from Spain to the Middle East where Israel is located. They also controlled most of Northern Africa. Their empire was the greatest in the world at that time.

There was a law in the empire that said that Roman soldiers could make the children that lived in the area carry their equipment packs for one mile from their houses.

In his teachings, Jesus said, "If someone forces you to go one mile, go with him two miles." (Matt. 5:41 NIV) Going the extra mile is what he was talking about. That is what the quote refers to.

Many people do only what is required by their parents, teachers, or bosses. They do as little as possible to just get by. It sure is easier than putting in extra work, isn't it? But the quote and Jesus are talking about a little extra effort.

In other words, do more than the bare minimum. Success in anything is going to take extra work. There was an Olympic swimmer that won several medals. When he was asked how he did it, he said that he spent 15 minutes extra each day swimming laps. After everyone else got out of the pool and went home, he stayed a little longer. There wasn't a crowd while he was going the extra mile. He had the pool to himself.

That's what it means that there isn't a crowd on the extra mile. Most people have stopped because they did only what they had to do. Now you are alone doing just a little more. But that is the way to be successful at anything. Do you want to be a great basketball player? Soccer player? Dancer? Guitar player? Writer? Scientist? Whatever you want to do, go the extra mile. At practice, be the one working the hardest. Be the one practicing at home a few minutes extra each day. At school, be the one listening to the teacher and asking questions to understand better.

As you continue on your success journey, you'll see fewer and fewer people. They just aren't willing to go the extra mile.

"You will find true success in those efforts that captivate your heart and soul–Belief fuels passion and passion rarely fails."

What do you really love to do? What if you had a whole day to do whatever you wanted? What would you spend the time doing? I like racing. If I could spend the whole day doing anything, it would be racing. Racing captivates my heart and soul. I have a passion for it. That means I love it. It is a big part of my life. I don't have a racecar, but I'm working on it. I'm 34 years old, and I'm going back to a dream I had as a kid.

What is it for you? Whatever they are, those dreams will speed you down the road on your success journey. You will have passion to do what it takes. You won't mind going the extra mile to be the best. You will have fun in life if you can spend most of your time doing what you love.

Maybe you don't know yet. That's all right. As you start doing more things, look for those that you really enjoy. If you can make one of them what you do when you grow up, you'll be more successful and have more fun.

John Maxwell, one of the leading experts on success today, says that part of success is knowing your purpose in life. We are on this earth to do something great. What is something great? Whatever you find that inspires you. I love helping kids. That's why I became a teacher. A lot of people told me to learn about computers. Others told me that there isn't enough money in teaching. It didn't matter. It inspired me. I wanted to make a difference to kids. For me, that was something great. For others it is being a full-time mom. Many people don't think that is fulfilling. For those moms, it is the best thing in the world. Finding and doing what you were put here for makes you a success. Start looking for it now. Your interests may change over time, and that's okay. If one sticks with you over time, that may be something to pay attention to.

You will have to do some things that you don't want to do, or don't like doing. That's life. Many people have to do the things they don't like most of the time. Do you think that their lives are fun? That's why they don't go the extra mile. Why would they do more of what they don't like?

Find something that you love to do. The passion you feel for that activity will not fail you. It will make your success journey a great adventure.

"The distance between success and failure can only be measured by one's desire."

Mark Spitz was an Olympic swimmer in 1968. He was a teenager and won a few medals. He was disappointed by his results. He told the reporters that he would be back in four years and win seven gold medals in seven different events. The reporters thought he was bragging.

Mark went home and trained for several hours a day in the pool to be ready for the next Olympic games in 1972. He came to the games confident of his success. He had said that he would win seven gold medals, and that was exactly what he intended to do.

He succeeded in his goal. He won seven gold medals and set several world records at the same time. What was the difference between success and failure? It was his desire to succeed.

The people who have a successful journey are the ones who really want to succeed—I mean really want to. If you asked a hundred people if they want to be successful, one hundred people would say, "Yes." If you asked them what they were doing to make sure they were successful, very few of them would have an answer. They don't have the desire to put in the extra that it takes.

So far it sounds like being successful is hard work. It is work. Nothing valuable comes easily. But the rewards are great. You'll look back at your life and know that you made a difference. You won't say, "I wish I would have...," because you did it. You took your chances and made the most of them. That's a life worth living!

"Success is the sum of small efforts repeated day in and day out."

Habits are those things we do without thinking about them. They are things that we do automatically. We learn habits. For example, you probably put your clothes on in the same order each day. You start with underwear (giggle, giggle), then pants and shirt. Finally you put on your sock and shoes. You probably even put on the same sock first each day. That is a habit.

You can develop a habit of doing your best and going the extra mile on things you do, or you can develop the habit of just getting by. The habit will be strengthened each time you choose.

It is important to start good habits now. The longer you do something the easier it is to do. If you start now doing your best on everything you do, it will get easier to put in the extra effort needed to succeed next time. The opposite is also true. If you start a habit now of just doing enough to get by, it will be easier to do it next time too.

I had created a habit of thinking that I was a failure. I knew I would fail at anything new that I tried to do. So I never tried anything new. I had created a habit of listening to the negative messages that were hitting me from every direction. It is hard for me to change those habits after twenty-eight years. It is hard to change your thinking after that long. I am trying to change the thoughts by changing the messages I am listening to. It happens one thought at a time. Each time I choose to listen to a positive message, it gets easier the next time.

Now I am writing a book. That is risky. Most authors get their first books rejected several times before it gets published. I am learning to take risks. It is a new habit I am trying to form.

You have a chance now to start a good habit of looking for positive messages. You have the chance to start doing your best in everything. It will become a habit that will help you on your journey.

The success journey isn't taken in giant leaps. It is a journey of small steps taken each and every day.

"Far better it is to dare mighty things, to win glorious triumphs, even though checkered by failure, than to take rank with those poor spirits who neither enjoy nor suffer much, because they live in the gray twilight that knows neither victory nor defeat."

—Theodore Roosevelt (26th President of the United States)

What if the only thing you ever succeeded at was doing nothing? What a sad life that would be. There would never be the thrill of winning a big game. There would never be the excitement of not knowing what would happen next.

President Roosevelt says that in this quote. Look at the parts of it. "Far better is it to dare mighty things, to win glorious triumphs, even though checkered by failure..." He means that life is so much better when you are challenging yourself to do great things with your life. Life is really worth living when you win big. That means that you overcome a fear and succeed. It means that you try something that is hard for you and succeed. It means that you do something great with your life. Will you fail on your way to success? You bet. But failures are stepping-stones to success.

The last part of the quote describes a life with no excitement. "... than to take rank with the poor souls who neither enjoy nor suffer much, because they live in the gray twilight that knows neither victory nor defeat." There was no TV when Theodore Roosevelt was alive. If there had been, he might have said," ...than to sit on the couch with those poor souls who neither enjoy nor suffer much unless their favorite character on TV does, who live in front of the TV five hours a night and know nothing but the TV show world they live in."

He is describing people with no joy in life. Too many adults give the best hours of the day to their boss (I know, you give your best hours to school). When they get home, there is no energy left to play with the kids. They want to sit and relax in front of the TV or newspaper. That is not a life that inspires people. That is not a life on a success journey.

Dare to do great things. You may fail. But that's better than never knowing the thrill of victory. You must dare to win or you will fail to live.

"Success is relative: It is what we can make of the mess we have made of things."
—T.S. Elliot

In the next section we will look at failure in more detail. This quote, once again, shows how failure is right there with success. You can't have success without some failure. They go together like peanut butter and jelly. In fact, do you like peanut butter by itself? Very few people do. Jelly makes the peanut butter better (Say that three times fast!).

It's like that with failure and success. Success tastes sweeter when it has some failure mixed with it. You enjoy an accomplishment more when you have had to win some battles along the way.

Have you messed up? Today? We all have. I mess up. The President messes up. Your parents mess up. Your teachers, friends, and you mess up. It is part of life. A person who can make something good come out of the mess he made will be successful.

You have probably heard someone tell you to learn from your mistakes. That is great advice. If you learn a lesson from it, it will be easier not to make the mistake again.

As a matter of fact, I am sitting here writing after I just messed up and lost my temper with my son. I got upset and yelled at him. I was mean the way I talked to him. Was I successful as a father? Of course not! But, as I realized I was wrong, I stopped yelling. I took his hand and apologized to him. We ended up hugging and laughing when I left his room. I guess I made something of the mess I made, so I was a successful father.

Did I learn a lesson from that situation? I hope so. I hope

that the next time a situation like that happens, I can settle down before I blow it.

Don't fear failure. It is the jelly that makes the success so much better.

"Success is going from failure to failure with great enthusiasm." –Winston Churchill

This quote is a lot like the last one. Failure is a step on the success journey. A successful person goes from failure to failure with a good attitude. Does it mean that you should try to fail and be happy about it? Of course not! You don't have to be happy about failing at anything. You just have to know that you will fail, learn from it, and keep moving forward on your journey.

The enthusiasm you feel as you go from failure to failure is the pride in yourself because you got up. Each time you get up and keep going after you fail gives you more strength for the next time. You believe in yourself more. You feel more confident in taking bigger risks. If you risk more, you might fail more. If you fail more, you will eventually be succeeding at greater and greater things.

So, have the right attitude as you travel down the road. The winning attitude will help you through the tough times.

"The greatest detriment to tomorrow's success is today's success." —John Maxwell

Way to go! You've finally done it! You kept at it until you succeeded! That is awesome! Now beware. The biggest danger to succeeding tomorrow is that hard-fought victory you won today.

That is what the quote talks about. The biggest thing that will keep you from success tomorrow is your success today. Isn't that wrong? Shouldn't it say that the biggest threat to tomorrow's success would be more failure? No. Today's success can threaten tomorrow's success. Let me explain.

Have you ever noticed that very few sports teams repeat as champions two times in a row? Why is that? There are lots of reasons. One of them is that they succeed today, and they don't plan ahead to succeed tomorrow.

Many sports teams don't change anything the next season after winning the championship. Why should they? They have the same players that proved they were the best last season. Shouldn't they be the best this season too? They do the same things that they did last year and expect the same results. It sounds good.

But the other teams have been training. They have brought in new people to improve the team. They have studied the champion's every move and figured out ways to beat them. All the other teams have moved forward. The champions have stayed the same. It is a bigger fight for them to stay on top.

Some people are like that too. If they win a battle, they think the war is over. If they finally overcome something, they think the struggle is over. If they do something great, they think that it is enough success to last them for a while.

You might study for a science test and get them all correct. That is a great accomplishment. Congratulations! But will getting them all correct on this test mean that you will get them all correct on the next test? Of course not. You can't stop studying for other tests because of your success on this one.

The truth is that when each day is over, all that you did that day is over too. If you failed at something, you have a new day to try again. If you succeed at something, you have a new day for new and greater challenges.

Use each success as a building block. Remember them to give you confidence in yourself. It will help you when things get tough. Celebrate each success. It is great that you did it. But then let it go so you can look ahead to the next challenge.

"Genius (success) is one percent inspiration and ninety-nine percent perspiration."
—Thomas Edison

Thomas Edison invented the light bulb, record players, motion pictures and thousands of other things. His quote means that most of success is hard work. Only a small part of success is having a good idea.

A good example of this is when he invented the light bulb. At that time, candles and oil lamps lighted houses, streets, and buildings. Edison knew that there was a better way. He worked for several years trying to find the right thing to put in a light bulb to make light. As electricity goes through the filament in the bulb, it gets hot and glows. That's why light bulbs are hot and give light.

Thomas tried thousands of different materials for the filament. Some would burn for a few seconds, while others would burn for only a few hours. He even tried a human hair! One time someone told him they were sorry the tests were failing. Thomas smiled and said, "We haven't failed. Now we know a thousand things that won't work, so we're that much closer to finding what will."

It was only through hard work that he successfully found something that worked. One day he tried some cotton thread. It burned for an hour, then two, then into the night. Thomas Edison stayed up watching it to the early hours of the morning. He knew he had found something. He kept improving on it. Because of his hard work and his will to keep going when it seemed like he might never find the answer, our world was changed. The age of electricity was born.

Work for the things you want. It may take some time to get them. Other people may think you are wasting your time and feel sorry for you. But when you see a light bulb, remember the attitude that Thomas Edison had. Each time something didn't work wasn't a failure; it was a step on his road to success.

"The only place where success comes before work is in a dictionary" —Vidal Sassoon

You have to work at being successful. We have seen that in all of the quotes so far. You have to look for positive messages to fill your mind. They don't just jump out and bite you like negative messages do.

It takes a strong will to do well in anything. You really

have to want it. Let's take school for example. The students who do well in school really want to. It is important to them. If school isn't important to you, why not? Even if you don't think the things you are doing are important, there are reasons your teacher has you do them.

One of the best things about doing your best and trying harder than others is that it creates a habit for you. We have already talked about how important it is to develop the right habits to help you on the success journey.

Find the things that you like to do. Make them part of your journey. Even if they are just fun activities, we need to keep life fun. As you grow you will start to see the things you are talented at. Use those things to speed you on your journey.

What is the opposite of success? Most people would say failure. That shows wrong understanding about what failure is. Now that you understand something about success, we need to explore what failure is and how it helps us on our success journey.

Chapter 2

Failure

We know that success is knowing the plan for your life and doing it. As you get older, the plan will get clearer if you look for it. Success is getting up and going on after you've fallen. Success is hard work.

But what about failure? Is it the opposite of success? If you don't succeed have you failed? John Maxwell says that understanding failure is what separates average people from people who do great things.

Most people see failure as doing something wrong. They tried something but it didn't work. They raised their hand to give the answer, but the teacher said that their answer wasn't correct. They blew it. They may try again, or they may quit. People are embarrassed when they do something wrong or give the wrong answer. Many people think that the answer is not to try again. They refuse to raise their hand again to answer the question in case they might be wrong.

Mark Twain said, " If a cat sits on a hot stove, he won't sit on a hot stove again." That is like the person who tries something that doesn't work and vows never to try it again. He went on to say, "He (the cat) won't sit on a cold stove either. He just doesn't like stoves." This is like the person that never tries anything again. He is afraid of failure. If he never tries anything difficult he can't fail at it. He lives a safe life. There is no success in that kind of life.

In a book called *Failing Forward*, John Maxwell says that

people who succeed look at failure differently than most people. Successful people don't think that *they* are a failure when they do something that doesn't work or make a mistake. They know that failing or making a mistake is just an unsuccessful try at something. They find out what went wrong. Then they change something and try again. Just like Thomas Edison did while looking for the right material for the light bulb.

These quotes will help you understand failure. If you understand it in the right way you can face it with the right attitude. Failing will actually be a stepping-stone to your success!

ॐ

"The credit belongs to those people who are actually in the arena...who know the great enthusiasms; the great devotions to a worthy cause; who at best, know the triumph of high achievement; and who, at worst, fail while daring greatly...so that their place shall never be with those cold and timid souls who know neither victory nor defeat."

–Theodore Roosevelt

This quote is very similar to the other quote from Theodore Roosevelt in the Success section. He is talking about success and failure in this one. He is praising the people who are working hard for something important to them. Those are the great enthusiasms and worthy causes. It is about people who are working to be successful.

The best thing about those people is that they know what it's like to do their best and achieve something important to them. The worst that could happen is that they, "fail while daring greatly." Is it such a bad thing to fail while you are trying to do something? No! You are at least willing to try. Those people who have failed and have given up aren't even trying any more. You are way ahead of them.

President Roosevelt goes on to say that when you fail, you will never be in the same place as "those cold and timid souls who know neither victory nor defeat." If someone is afraid to try, he will not fail. That is true. He won't ever win either. There is no excitement in a life like that. It leaves his soul cold and timid. He has no confidence in himself.

Getting the wrong answer isn't fun. It is embarrassing in class isn't it? Remember, I am a teacher. Let me tell you, if you got it wrong there were probably other kids whose answers were way off too. They were just afraid to raise their hand. Besides, if your answer was wrong, it only means that you have the chance to learn the right answer.

I always tell my students that learning is just tweaking your thinking. You have an idea about a topic. Your idea may be close to correct but have one little thing that needs tweaking. For example, many students think that *all* spiders have eight eyes. The book we read about spiders says that *some* spiders have eight eyes. Other spiders have six, four, or two eyes. They were almost correct that *all* spiders have eight eyes. We tweak our thinking and say that *some* spiders have eight eyes. Now our thinking is more correct and we have learned something.

That is what failure can do. It points out where you need to tweak your thinking or the way you do something to get the right answer or results.

If you aren't afraid to "fail while daring greatly," you will always be learning and improving your skills and knowledge. Those failures can move you on the success journey if you learn from them. When you learn a lesson from mistakes, you fail *forward* toward what you are trying to accomplish.

"It is hard to fail, but it is worse never to have tried to succeed." –Theodore Roosevelt

That quote is pretty easy to understand, isn't it? Failing isn't supposed to be fun. It isn't something you should enjoy. It is hard to fail. No one likes it. But winners realize that it will happen and they *choose* to learn from it.

President Roosevelt also said that even though failure is hard, it is worse not to have tried to succeed. If you give up trying you become a person with a "cold and timid soul" like he talks about in the last quote.

If you want to be good at something, you will have to

go through a period of doing it poorly. Think of the greatest athletes or musicians. They had to go through a period of doing things wrong before they got good. If you don't believe me, just ask a famous musician's mom if her son or daughter could always play so well. Remember, Mom was there to hear all of the practicing when he was just getting started. Ask any star athlete's first coaches if they thought this person would be a great star someday. The coach knew him when he could hardly catch the ball.

Don't let that period of failure stop you from trying. Success is on the way. Keep learning from the mistakes and you will improve. Look for improvement, not perfection.

There is no perfection. A baseball player is considered a success (a great hitter) at the plate if they get on base one out of every three times at bat. That means they fail two times out of every three tries.

Keep trying and failing and learning and growing. Success is on the way if you keep improving.

"Half the failures in life arise from pulling in one's horse as he is leaping."
—Julius C. Hare and Augustus Hare

To make a horse stop, the rider pulls back on the reigns. This pulls back on the horse's head. Over a period of time, the horse learns that pulling back on the reigns is a signal to stop.

Have you ever seen a horse and rider jumping over something? They charge at the obstacle and sail over it as the horse leaps. What would happen if the rider pulled back on the reigns just before the horse started to jump? The horse would try to stop. They would probably crash into the obstacle. That would hurt and they would avoid doing that again in the future. Now they are afraid of failure.

Maybe you'll understand this example better. Have you seen the skateboarders, roller bladers, trick bike riders, and motocross riders doing their flips and spins and tricks in the air? It is amazing what they can do. Do you think they succeeded the first time? How many times do you think they fell learning to do those stunts?

What would happen to the motocross rider if he charged up the hill to make a jump and put on the breaks at the top of the ramp? Ouch! What about a skater who is ready to jump up on the rail to do a grind, but then gets scared of falling and doesn't jump? He would get hurt wouldn't he? It would be easier to be afraid next time too. Each time it happened he would be more afraid of trying. Soon, he wouldn't try at all and might even give up skating.

That is what happens to people who don't try to get over the walls they face. If someone quits instead of trying to do what may be hard, it will be harder for him or her to try the next time. Over time they might just be afraid to fail. Then they don't try at all.

The quote says that half of failures are when people don't try to get past the obstacle between them and success. They quit instead.

When you see the wall up ahead, don't be afraid of it. Go at it and try to get over it anyway. Will you always get over on the first try? Of course not. See what went wrong, and try something a little different the next time. Keep leaping walls and soon you'll think you are Superman or Superwoman!

"Many of life's failures are people who did not realize how close they were to success when they gave up."

—Thomas Edison

A lot of people give up too soon. This book is a great example. I am working on it and everything is going great. I write a little each day. It is getting closer to being done each time I write. I am encouraged by the progress. Each time I sit and write, it gets easier.

Today I talked to a friend who has had four books published. I asked him for some tips about what to do. He told me that it is pretty hard to get a publisher to even look at what I have. How many publishers will I have to talk to before I find one who wants to publish the book? I don't know. But I know that I will always ask one more. I'm not going to give up until I succeed.

What if I got discouraged and quit sending it to publishers? The next one on the list could have been the one that wanted it. You never know how close you are to success. You can't afford to give up. The next time could be the winner.

The greatest basketball player ever almost gave up too soon. Did you know that Michael Jordan was cut from his high school basketball team? He wasn't good enough to make a team of 15-year-olds. He went home and was very disappointed and sad. He was ready to quit. This failure was hard for him. His mother told him not to let this stop him from reaching his goals. She told him to turn the negative energy into positive energy and keep working. He could try out again next year.

He worked out all year to improve. He did try out again and made the team. The rest is history.

If you want to succeed, never, ever give up. You may be just one more try from success.

"The things which hurt, instruct."
–Benjamin Franklin

This quote means that the things that cause pain will teach us something. It doesn't mean physical pain only, like when you fall down. It means the pain of failure, embarrassment, or shame too. It is talking about failure. Someone else said the same thing this way, "The gem cannot be polished without friction, nor man perfected without trials (failures)."

When you fail, it can be painful. Maybe you studied for a long time for a test and still got a bad grade. That hurts. Learn from it. What can you do differently next time? Maybe you spent a lot of time, but you were in front of the TV with cartoons on. Do you see something that could be changed next time?

I played soccer in college. In the last game of the regular season I yelled at the referee and told him he was an idiot. Oops! He gave me a red card. I had to leave the game, and I would miss our next game. Our next game was the first playoff game. If we won, we would play again. If we lost, we were done for the season.

We played against a team we should have killed. We couldn't score at all. It was a 0–0 tie. The game went into overtime. Neither team could score after 120 minutes of play. It was still 0–0. Then it went to a penalty kick shootout. Each team picked five players to take a shot from 12 yards out. Only the goalie was there to try and stop it. After all five from each team took their shots, it was tied 3–3. It went to sudden death. The first team to miss would lose the whole game and be done for the year. I think we finally won in the seventh or eighth round.

What's the point of that story? That experience hurt. I had to be the ball boy for that whole game, overtime, shootout, and sudden death. It was killing me. Because of the pain, I learned an important lesson. I never yelled at a referee again! It was a lesson I couldn't learn without the pain of missing that game.

Sure I blew it when I lost my temper and got the red card. But I was able to learn an important lesson from the experience. I have never gotten a red card since then. The pain was able to instruct me, but I had to be willing to learn the lesson.

Don't let the pain just hurt. It's trying to help you. If you are going to feel the pain, wouldn't it be smart to get something good from it too?

"You cannot go back and make a brand new start, but you can start to make a brand new end."

–John Maxwell

John Maxwell is one of the top teachers on being a leader. I heard this quote on a tape of him speaking to a large crowd. It gave me the courage to start changing myself.

The past has passed. Yesterday is over. There is nothing you can do to change yesterday. You can't go back to yesterday, or any other time in the past, and change it. What's done is done. But...today is a different story. You are given today as a gift to do something with. What will you do with it? Will you use it to make you a better person? Or will you sit and watch TV all day? How will you invest today?

To invest something means that it gets more valuable over time. Will today add value to your life in the future? Will it make you a better person in the future? Will the things you do today make your life better tomorrow? That is what I mean by adding value to your life. Will today be a valuable part of your life, or will you just spend it? To spend something means to use it up so it is gone. When today is gone it will either be something of value or just wasted time. You choose which it will be.

Today, you can start to make a brand new end. That is the future. Have you been just spending your days with no thought to the future? The future is time that will come: tomorrow, next week, next month, next year, ten years from now, and 40 years from now. What you do today can make the future better. What you do today can also make the future the same as today. Which will you choose?

Does this mean you can't play or have any fun? Of course not. You are a kid. Playing is part of your job. But don't forget that the other part of your job is learning. Make sure you learn something each day that makes you a better person. Add positive messages to your life each day, and the day will be a wise investment in your future.

A failure is a man who has blundered, but is not able to cash in on the experience.

–Elbert Hubbard

Learn from your mistakes. Have you ever heard that before? If you haven't, let me be the first to tell you. The best thing about a mistake is that you get to learn something from it. You have to look for the lesson. Most times it doesn't jump out and bite you.

Let me tell you about a man that didn't cash in on the mistakes he made. Do you know who the Wright Brothers are? They were the bicycle mechanics that never went to college but were the first to fly in an airplane! There was another man trying to do the same thing. His name was Dr. Samuel P. Langley. He wasn't a doctor that could help if you got sick. He was a guy that went to school for a VERY long time to be the best in his field. He had been doing experiments with wings and large model airplanes for nearly ten years. He was having a lot of success.

He got $50,000 from the government to build a plane that would carry a man. That had never been done before. He worked for two years and successfully tested a gasoline-powered model. It was time to try it with a man flying the plane. On October 8, 1903 he attempted the first flight. As the plane took off, part of it got caught on something and the plane fell apart after flying 50 feet. The newspapers made fun of Langley in the next day's papers. But he didn't let that stop him.

Only eight weeks later he was ready to try again. He had redesigned the part that broke the first time. But as the new plane was launched, a cable that held the wing up broke, and the plane crashed again. This time, he didn't come back. The newspaper articles made fun of him again, and he let them get to him. He quit. After years of success, he let two failures stop him. He wasn't able to cash in on the experience. He failed.

A few days later, on December 17, 1903, the Wright brothers flew in the first plane for only a minute. It went only 850 feet. They had been trying for a while too. They had some successes and some failures. Each success taught them what worked. Each failure taught them what didn't work. They cashed in on the failures and reached their goal. But they didn't stop there. They kept experimenting and improving their design. In 1905 they flew for a half an hour and went 24 miles. Their names became famous. Dr. Samuel P. Langley had a stoke and died three years later. Most school children know the Wright Brothers, but only a few remember Langley.

Learn from your mistakes. They can be great lessons that lead to great success!

"It is better to attempt something great and fail than to attempt nothing and succeed."
–Dr. Robert Schuller

There is one thing you don't want to succeed at. You don't want to succeed at doing nothing! " Yeah, I remember Matt. He never really did anything with his life." That would be the saddest thing to ever hear at a funeral. "Matt was good for one thing in this company...nothing." When you move away, wouldn't you like people to remember the great things about you?

What would you like people to remember about you when you are gone? Have you ever seen a gravestone? It has the person's name and the date they were born and died. Between those dates is a dash. The dash is the person's life. That is all you know about a person from a grave stone. But somewhere out there are people who remember the person. What do they remember most about the person? Do they remember that he was always trying? He may have failed along the way, but he never gave up. Is their strongest memory that he never tried because he was afraid to fail? Wouldn't that be terrible if that was all people remembered about your life?

Remember Mr. Langley and the failed attempts at flying?

Sure he gave up and quit when it got tough. But he at least tried. The people who made fun of him were on the sidelines. They were safely to the side and didn't face the dangers that the guy in the plane faced. At least Langley attempted great things and failed. The critics have all succeeded at nothing. Who deserves the credit?

Don't let your dash be wasted. Attempt great things with your life. Remember that great things are things that you feel are worth doing. Find your talents and then find something that lets you use your talents. You'll be good at it and enjoy it. There will be things that are hard and that you fail at along the way. It is better to at least try than to do nothing and be good at it.

Failure is not something that you can avoid. If you try something new, you will probably not be good at it right away. No one ever is. Keep trying, failing, changing something, and trying again. That will help you get better at it. Eventually you will be good. You've heard people say that "practice makes perfect." That isn't true. Remember the baseball players who only get a hit one out of three tries. Some of them have been playing for 30 years. They still aren't perfect. Practice does make better. That's all you can expect.

Failure is not the end of the road on your success journey; it is the on-ramp to the highway of success! If you see failure as just a way to learn what doesn't work, like Thomas Edison and the light bulb, you will actually do better, faster than if you think failure is the end of the line.

Chapter 3

Attitude

The best thing about all of this so far is that it is a choice. We choose how we look at failure. We choose to go on. Having a positive attitude is a must. And the attitude you have is also a choice. Sure there are days when you may be sick and feel horrible. But that is how you *feel*. You can still have a good attitude. You can choose not to be grumpy and whiny. You have the same choice when you fail.

When my kids want to whine and fuss, I tell them to go to their rooms. If they want to choose a bad attitude, they can. I just don't want it around me.

Your attitude can lift you up as a person, or it can pull you down. The choice is yours. Someone once said, "The currents that determine our dreams and shape our lives flow from the attitudes we nurture everyday." The thoughts and actions we have each day come from the attitude we have. This starts a chain reaction that I will describe later. Bad things lead to more bad things, or good things lead to more good things. You choose which happens by your attitude. Choose wisely.

W.W. Ziege said, "Nothing can stop the man with the right mental attitude from achieving his goal; nothing on earth can help the man with the wrong mental attitude." If you want to go far in life, you simply must have the right attitude. If you don't, there is nothing that can help you succeed. Your bad attitude just won't make it possible.

"Our lives are not determined by what happens to us, but how we react to what happens; not by what life brings us, but by the attitude we bring to life. A positive attitude causes a chain reaction of positive thoughts, events, and outcomes. It is a catalyst...a spark that creates extraordinary results. It is a little thing that makes a BIG difference."

This is one of my favorite quotes. It explains the story of the twin brothers with the alcoholic father from the introduction. The attitudes of the two men made their lives go in different directions. Remember the story? One had a drinking problem and a bad family life. The other became president of a large company. They both had the same answer when they were asked why they ended up where they were in life. Both men said that they ended up where they were because of the effect their father had on them.

One brother used it as an excuse to fail. He chose to have a bad attitude. He felt that he would end up as an alcoholic too because that's all he saw of his father. He made a poor choice.

His brother was living proof of what the quote says. He was not going to let his life just happen. He became the president of a company on purpose. His life wasn't determined by what happened to him but by how he reacted to what happened. In other words, he didn't let what happened to him as a kid affect his future. By choosing not to use his past as an excuse, he chose to win instead. His reaction was to be positive.

His positive attitude caused "a chain reaction of positive thoughts, events, and outcomes." Every time he chose positive thoughts, like "I'm a winner," it set him up for positive actions. He did good things because he felt like a winner. For example, choosing to study instead of watching TV made him do well on his schoolwork. This made him feel like a winner, which made him study more. This made him do well in school, which made him feel like a winner. See how the loop gets going? This is a chain reaction. Once it starts, it is hard to stop.

Unfortunately, it is also true the other way. A bad attitude causes a negative chain reaction of thoughts, actions, and outcomes. Let's look at the same example. His brother reacted to their father with a bad attitude. He felt like it wasn't fair. You know what, it isn't fair. Everyone should have a loving family that makes a person feel special. That's the way families were made to work. But, people make bad choices that ruin the plan sometimes. It may not be fair. It may be hard. You'll just have to decide to have a good attitude anyway. Talk to another adult you trust. They can help you feel special. Let me tell you–You are special!

But, back to the example. If the boy chooses to have a bad attitude about his life, he may feel like a loser. If he feels like a loser, he may think that he'll never do well in school anyway, so he doesn't study. Because he didn't study, he will do poorly on his work or test. When he gets a bad grade on a paper he feels like a loser, so why should he study? If he doesn't study, he'll get a bad grade, which makes him feel like a loser. The loop has started, and it's hard to stop.

Your attitude is a little thing that makes a BIG difference in your life. Be careful to keep a good attitude. One way to help is to feed your mind positive things. If you put good things in your mind, you tend to get good things back out. What are good things you can put in your mind? Read positive books like this. Watch educational TV shows. Hang around positive people. Look for positive things to fill your mind with. It will have a huge impact on your life. Start now while you are young. Remember how I said I have had to fight against 30 years of negative messages in my mind? It sure is a lot harder as you get older. If you get nothing else from this book remember this: Your attitude is your most important weapon to protect you from negative messages. Guard it with your life. It's that important!

"Your attitude almost always determines your altitude in life." –John Maxwell

Your attitude leads to success. Your attitude leads to failure. You choose. How far you go in life is based on your attitude.

Altitude is how high up a plane, bird, rocket, or mountain is. This quote is saying that your attitude will make you fly high in life or crawl on the ground. Flying or crawling is your altitude, or how high you get in life.

Roger Crawford is an author and speaker. He used to be a professional tennis player too. His attitude allowed him to fly high in his life. Oh, by the way, he has no hands and only one foot!

Roger was born with only stumps for arms and one foot. His parents always told him that he could do anything he wanted in life. They let him know he was loved and accepted for who he was. His father told him that he was only as handicapped as he wanted to be. They encouraged him to try whatever he wanted. They also made sure he kept a positive attitude. They never let him feel sorry for himself. What a great gift they gave him.

In college he played tennis on the team. After college he actually became a pro tennis player! He was certified by the U.S. Tennis Association. His attitude let him soar like an eagle!

One day he got a phone call from someone that had read about him and wanted to meet him. They met at a local restaurant. When the man arrived they shook hands. Roger was surprised that the man's hands were almost the same as his! He was excited because he seemed to have found someone like himself for a friend. As they talked, Roger soon discovered that this was not the kind of person he wanted to hang around with. This man had a bad attitude. He blamed every failure in his life on having no hands. Even though he admitted that he was late to work a lot and called in sick often, he thought that he got fired because of his handicap. He blamed his condition for every failure. He kept himself crawling on the ground instead of soaring like Roger.

Please don't walk away from someone with a bad attitude... Run! Attitudes are like getting a cold. Someone else's bad attitude can make your good attitude sick. Stay away! That's why I walk away from my kids or make them go into their rooms if they want to have a bad attitude. I don't want their negative attitude to change my positive attitude. Stay away.

Protect your attitude. It's your most important weapon to beat the grumpies!

"The greatest discovery of any generation is that a human being can alter his life by altering his attitude."

Your attitude has the ability to change your life. Michael Jordan was disappointed and upset after getting cut from the high school basketball team. He changed his attitude, and it changed his life. Roger Crawford changed his attitude. He didn't let his handicap ruin his life. He changed his attitude, and it changed his life. Samuel P. Langley changed his attitude after failing to get his plane off the ground. He changed his attitude, and it changed his life. So it works both positively and negatively.

If someone asked you if you had a good attitude or bad attitude most of the time, what would you say? It's an important question to think about. Your attitude has the power to change your way of looking at things. A good attitude leads to positive actions and outcomes that lead to a better attitude. It starts a chain reaction. A bad attitude leads to negative actions and outcomes, which give you more of a bad attitude. And so on, and so on, and so on.

You don't just choose your attitude once. It is something you must choose each minute. It becomes a habit as you consistently choose to react in a positive way. Judith K. Knowlton said, "I discovered I always have choices and sometimes it's only a choice of attitude." No matter what happens to you in your life, you have the power to choose. Maybe what happens is out of your control, but you still have the power to choose your attitude.

Have you heard the story of Apollo 13? It was the third mission to the moon. When the space ship was about 200,000 miles from home, an explosion rocked the ship. They started leaking oxygen into space. You don't want to be 200,000 miles in space without oxygen.

The explosion was out of their control, but the men had a choice. They could have reacted with anger at their circumstances. That might have led to fighting, then other mistakes, then to failure, and even their deaths.

They could have reacted with despair and given up hope of ever returning to earth. Then they wouldn't have done the things that needed to be done in order to get home. Their bad attitude toward their situation could have led to bad decisions, then to bad actions, which would have given bad results. The bad results would have given them a worse attitude leading them to bad decisions, and bad results. The cycle would keep repeating until they died in space.

During this crisis the men of mission control and the astronauts had to invent new ways of doing things. The lunar module was the only ship with power and oxygen. But it was only designed to last about 40 hours. The problem was that they were 90 hours from home. They had to invent ways to make the equipment last until they could get home.

Fortunately, no one ever gave up. The astronauts, Jim Lovell, Fred Haise, and Jack Swigert, and the men at mission control kept a positive attitude. Gene Kranz, the man in charge at mission control told all the men on the ground working for him that, "failure is not an option." They chose a good attitude. That led to good decisions, actions, and results. Each good result improved their attitude which helped them make good decisions the next time. Good decisions led to positive action, which gave good results. The cycle was a positive one that led to success. They made it back to earth safely.

Start choosing to have a good attitude now, no matter what. It will become a habit. Your attitude could someday be a matter of life or death. Would you like to test how good you are at choosing a good attitude when it is that important?

"Whether you think you can, or think you can't...you're right." —Henry Ford

Henry Ford made cars in the early 1900s. A lot of other people made cars too. At that time, only a few people worked on each car. It took a long time and cost a lot of money. Only wealthy people had cars.

Ford worked out a way to build a car on an assembly line that used a lot of workers. Each worker was responsible for a specific job on each car. They got better at it and could do the job faster. Now Ford could produce many cars each day and each one was cheaper. He called his car the Model T. Most people laughed at him. They thought that the cars wouldn't be as good.

Ford believed in his idea, so he worked as if he knew it would work. He did things with a good attitude. He did the things necessary for success. His good attitude started a chain reaction of thoughts, actions, and outcomes that led to success and a better attitude.

He said that if you believe, or have a good attitude, in what you are doing, you will succeed. He also said that if you believe that what you are doing won't work, it won't. Your unbelief, or bad attitude, will start a bad chain reaction of thoughts, actions and outcomes that leads to failure.

Your belief, or attitude, in what you are doing is an important part of how it turns out. Ford believed his idea. In a few years, the number of cars on the road went from a few thousand to millions. His belief in his idea changed the world!

There are now billions of cars in the world. It all started with belief and a positive attitude! Where can your belief take you?

"Our destiny is shaped by our thoughts and our actions. We cannot direct the wind, but we can adjust the sails."

Where we end up in the future comes from what we think and do. We can't control the things that happen to us, but we can control how we react to what happens. That is what the quote means.

Our thoughts are shaped by what we put into our brains. Computer programmers have a saying, "garbage in, garbage out." If the program they write is not well done, the program won't do what it is supposed to do. If the program they write is garbage, then it will give out garbage. It won't work.

Our brains are more complex than the fastest computer. They are like huge sponges. We absorb everything around us. Your brain absorbs things that you aren't even aware of. As you sit reading this, there are sounds that you hear that your brain processes and ignores because they aren't important. Your brain monitors the temperature. If you started to get cold while reading, your brain would recognize it and send you to get a sweater. If your brain sensed that you were hungry, it would make you get food...hey, come back. I didn't mean now!

What you put into your brain is very important. That's why you need to look for positive input. Like I said in the introduction, negative messages are all over the place. You don't have to look for them. They look for you. Finding positive messages takes effort. You have to search for them. Make a habit of looking for positive input for *your* computer each day. What you put in is what you'll get out. What you put in is the stuff your thoughts are made of. Let it be good!

Another reason for good input is that the thoughts that it makes will be the actions that come out. Your actions start with your thoughts. Good thoughts lead to positive action. The positive action leads to good results. The good results give you good feelings and more good thoughts. Remember the chain reaction? Good thoughts lead to good actions, but bad thoughts lead to bad actions too. Beware!

The wind is a natural force that no person can control. Do you know that a sailboat can sail almost directly into the wind? The sails can be moved so that the wind coming almost straight at the boat can actually push it forward. Sailors cannot direct the wind, but they can adjust the sails.

In life, we cannot control all the things that happen to us. Some things will be good, but some things will be bad. We have no control over most things. What we can control is our attitude. It's not what happens to us, but how we react to what happens. Successful people know that they can let hard times get them down and stop them, like Samuel P. Langley, or they can choose to move on, like Michael Jordan.

Make up your mind that whatever happens, you will have a good attitude. Someone once said that "if life gives you lemons, make lemonade." Make something good out of a bad situation. That can only happen with a great attitude. Someone else described a person with a great attitude as a person who could be standing in a room of horse manure (poo) and know that there's a pony in there somewhere. They were looking for the good thing in a room full of bad things.

When things happen, remember that you can only control one thing–your attitude. Fill your mind with good thoughts so you react with good actions. Be a pony finder!

"A bright attitude is the right attitude. It is a source of empowerment that can move everyone in the right direction."

1978 was a good year for the Wheaton North High School football team. They made it all the way to the sectional finals before they lost. It was the farthest they had ever gotten in the state tournament. Twenty of 22 players graduated that year. The next year's team was mostly young players.

The newspapers gave them no chance at even winning one game that year. They called it a "rebuilding year." That meant that everyone thought they would just be there on the field with the other team with no chance of winning. The first game of the season was close, and Wheaton had a chance to actually win at the end. They ended up losing 13-14.

In the locker room, the team thought the coach was going to chew them out for losing. To their surprise, the coach told them that he had never seen a team play so well. Yeah, they lost, but the coach said they were winners. He told the offensive line what a great job they did blocking. He talked about how well the defense played. He talked about the individual players. For twenty minutes he built up the players and the team. He told them that they could win the State Championship.

The coach had a bright attitude and passed it along to the players. It got them moving in the right direction. The players knew that the newspapers said that they would not even win a game. Now the coach was telling them that they could win the championship.

They won the next game. The papers thought they were lucky. They won the next game and the next and the next. Now the papers and students were saying that this team could end the season with more wins than losses. They won the next game and the next and the next. In fact, they won the rest of their games. They also won their conference.

In the first playoff game they played Simeon High School from Chicago. Wheaton North received the kick-off. The guy caught the ball, started running it back and got hit at the thirty-yard line. The ball popped out to a Simeon player who ran it in for a touchdown. They were down 7-0 after nine seconds.

Wheaton received the next kick-off and the exact same thing happened. After 15 seconds they were losing 14-0. On the next kick-off, the coach told the receiver to catch the ball and run it out of bounds. Wheaton never gave up and won that game 34-14. They won two more games and won the State Championship!

It all started with the coach's attitude. It gave power to the players and set them on fire. It started them in the right direction. They did what everyone thought was impossible because of the power of a bright attitude.

This story shows why a good attitude is so important. It sets you on the right path and can affect other people too. What could *you* do with the right attitude?

"Happiness is not a state to arrive at but, rather, a manner of traveling."

There is nothing that you can get or nothing you can do that will MAKE you happy. You won't all of a sudden get happy. Happiness is an attitude that you develop over time. Happiness happens when you have a winning attitude through your journey.

Happiness, like your attitude, is a choice. You have to choose to be happy when things don't go your way. You have to choose to have a good attitude when things don't go your way. Happiness is choosing to look for the pony in the room full of manure.

Do you like to be around people who look like they have just eaten a lemon? They look like they haven't smiled in twenty years. Or do you like to be around people who have a twinkle in their eyes and a smile on their face? They always look like they have just gotten a present. They laugh and smile all the time.

How do you work on your attitude? Hang around people who have good attitudes. Get positive input from good books. Talk to people who have good attitudes. Only watch positive things on TV. The Bible says, "Whatever is true, whatever is noble, whatever is right, whatever is pure, whatever is lovely, whatever is admirable–if anything is excellent or praiseworthy– think about such things." (Philippians 4:8)

As you surround yourself with positive things, your attitude will improve. As your attitude improves, you have a smile more often. When you smile more often, you will have happiness. It isn't something you get; it is an attitude you have because you are a winner!

"The pessimist sees difficulty in every opportunity. The optimist sees opportunity in every difficulty."

Pessimists are people who never see anything good in a situation. They see and smell the manure in the room. Optimists are the people looking for a pony.

Everything you do in life will have challenges. Nothing that is worth much comes easy. The writer Miguel de Cervantes said, "That which costs little is less valued." Pessimists look at an opportunity and see all of the hard things about it. It will take too much time. It will be too risky. The chance to fail is great. They have a hundred excuses why they shouldn't do it.

The optimist looks at something that looks hard and sees an opportunity to win. They see a chance to succeed. They see an opportunity to grow. They know that everything that happens, good or bad, can be an opportunity. Your attitude decides. When good things happen, it is easy to see the chance for something good to be the result. But when bad things happen only the optimists, people with good attitudes, find the way to make something good come from it.

Are people born a pessimist or an optimist? There is probably some of it wired into your makeup. But it is mostly learned. If your parents are worriers, chances are that you learned to worry. If they are risk takers, you probably learned to take risks too. The nice thing is that if you learned it, you can also unlearn it. It will take time and practice. You will have to choose to look for the good in all things instead of the bad. It won't be easy, but if you want to continue on your success journey, it is something you will have to do.

If you don't learn to look for the pony, the manure will get too deep and you will drown in it. Yuck!

"If you keep your face to the sunshine, you never see the shadows." –Helen Keller.

This is the first quote in the book from Helen Keller, but it's not the last. Do you know the story of this remarkable woman?

Helen Keller was born on June 27, 1880. She was growing

and learning like any other child. When she was about 18 months old she had a very high fever for many days. The doctor thought she might even die. One day she woke up and the fever was gone, but when the fever left her, Helen just lay in her crib. The sun was shining right in her eyes, but she didn't notice. Her mom waved her hand in front of Helen's eyes. She didn't even blink. Mrs. Keller knew that Helen was blind. A few days later, the bell rang to call the family to breakfast. Helen didn't move, and she always started toward the dining room when she heard the bell. Mrs. Keller picked up a rattle and rattled it right in Helen's ear. Helen didn't move. Mrs. Keller knew that Helen was also deaf.

Can you imagine not being able to see or hear anything? Maybe you've woken up in the middle of the night and it was totally dark and silent. That's what all of Helen's life was like. She grew and became more like an animal than a child. She would walk around the table and pick things up from other people's plates during meals. She would have tantrums if she didn't get what she wanted. Her parents felt sorry for her and gave in to her. They gave her whatever she wanted.

Once Helen found her baby sister in the cradle she used for her doll. She got so angry that she pushed the cradle on the floor with her sister in it. Another time she almost burned herself when she moved a wet apron too close to the fire. Her dress caught on fire and she started to scream. Someone in the next room was able to put it out before it burned her. Her parents were losing hope. Captain Keller, Helen's dad, was ready to send her away to a hospital where she would live out the rest of her life.

Instead, they heard of a school in Boston that had once taught a girl who was deaf-blind. They wrote a letter to the director of the school. He said he would send a teacher to try and help Helen. He sent Annie Sullivan to Alabama to be Helen's teacher. Helen was seven years old at this time.

Helen didn't like Annie at first. Annie didn't let Helen get her own way. Annie wouldn't let Helen eat things from her plate. One morning, Helen and Annie fought for over an hour.

Annie wouldn't let Helen eat unless she used a fork and spoon. They wrestled as Annie picked up Helen and carried her to pick up the spoon every time she threw it down. Then she would force her to scoop up food with the spoon instead of using her hands. It lasted all morning. Now Helen really hated Annie.

Annie kept trying to teach Helen that everything had a name. Helen knew that the wet stuff was for drinking, but she didn't know that it was called water. She could feel her doll and knew that it was like her with two eyes, a nose, a mouth, and two arms and legs, but she didn't know that it was called a doll.

Most deaf people use sign language to communicate with others. Helen couldn't see the sign language because she was blind. Blind people can still hear and speak. Helen couldn't because she was deaf too. Annie spelled words with her fingers into Helen's hand. Helen could feel what the shapes were. She even got good at copying the shapes of the letters. But, she didn't know what they meant.

This went on for a few months. She was good at copying Annie, but it was just a game to Helen. One day Annie knew that Helen needed to learn to behave. She would never learn to have manners and behave if she got everything she wanted because of her tantrums. Annie and Helen moved to the small house on the other side of the farm. Helen's parents weren't allowed to visit her. For a few weeks, things went on as usual. Helen and Annie played the hand games. Helen still had no idea what they meant.

One day in April, Annie and Helen were outside. Annie finger spelled the name of everything they touched into Helen's hand. She was doing it out of habit. She had almost given up hope that Helen would ever get it. They went to the water pump to get a drink. Annie pumped the water into Helen's hand and spelled w-a-t-e-r into her hand again. Suddenly Helen's face changed, as if she were trying to understand something. Annie saw the look and knew that Helen was on the edge of understanding. She pumped more water over their hands and spelled water again and again. Finally, Helen started to spell it back to her! She knew that the letters w-a-t-e-r meant the cool, wet stuff that she felt.

Helen ran around touching things and Annie spelled the names into her hand. Helen learned her name that day. For almost eight years she didn't even know her name. That day was the most important day in Helen's life. From that day on, she was like a sponge. She wanted to learn the names of everything. Annie took her to the beach, zoo, and circus so she could experience new things. She taught her how to read Braille. Braille is a way that blind people can read by touching raised bumps on the page. The bumps are in patterns that stand for letters. By feeling the bumps, a blind person can put the letters together into words. Helen loved to read because she could experience things that she would never get to do.

Helen went to college. Annie sat with Helen in her classes and finger spelled everything that the teacher said. After class, Helen would go to her Braille typewriter and type everything she could remember. Annie also had to read the other books to Helen. Annie would finger spell everything the books said to her. This is how Helen got through college. She graduated with honors in 1904. That means that she was one of the top students in her class.

While she was in college, she wrote a book called *The Story of My Life*. Helen and Annie went on after college to give speeches and write articles for many magazines. Helen traveled all over the world trying to make life better for blind people. She met many famous people and inspired millions of people in her life. She was a remarkable person. What was her attitude like? She was able to say, "If you keep your face to the sunshine, you never see the shadows." She knew that if you have a good attitude, the problems of life would not be so big. That's what she meant in the quote.

I told most of her story here because she is a great example of the power of a good attitude. There will be more quotes and stories about her later. Think about the obstacles she overcame to do what she did in her life. It makes some of my challenges look small when I compare them to hers. That helps me to keep going.

"On with the dance. Let the joy be unconfined. That is my motto. Whether there's anyone dancing, or not; if there's any joy to be unconfined, if I dance there will be a dance. If I am joyous, there will be joy." — Mark Twain

Mark Twain was an author in the late 1800s. As a matter of fact, he knew Helen Keller. They were good friends. She loved his stories called *Huckleberry Finn* and *Tom Sawyer*.

The quote is a great way to end the section about attitude. It simply means that your attitude is a choice. It doesn't depend on other things. He said that his motto was to dance and let his joy out for everyone to experience. That is what "let the joy be unconfined" means. He was going to have a great attitude and be joyful. That's how he chose to live his life.

It didn't matter if anyone chose to join him, or if anyone else was letting their joy out. That didn't matter to him because he knew that he was responsible for his own attitude and joy. That's not always easy to do. When other people have a bad attitude, it can bring us down too. When I get home from work and my son is in his room having a tantrum, it is so easy for me to get angry right away because I see that my wife is angry. It is hard to see this going on and come in with a good attitude to try to calm the situation. But that is what I must do. I must choose to be the one with a good attitude. Even if I can't fix the situation, I must keep my good attitude.

Your attitude is an important weapon. It can defeat the grumpies. It can slay the negative messages. It can turn failure into victory. It can wipe out those who say you can't. Use it every day to win the battles. Choose to dance when no one else is dancing. Choose to be joyful while everyone else is grumpy. You will succeed because you are a success! You are a warrior, male or female. You will win because you use your most powerful weapon—your attitude!

Chapter 4

Dreams and Goals

Your dreams and goals in life are like a compass for you. A compass shows you which direction you are traveling. It can be used to help you get to where you want to go. If you have a map, a compass can guide you. Your dreams and goals are like that.

Where do you want to go in life? Too many people don't have a clear idea of what they want their life to turn out like. They have no map or compass. They don't really need a map or compass because they are just taking the Road of Life where it leads them. They don't have a destination. The danger of traveling that way is that you might not like where you end up.

Don't get me wrong—you can't control everything in your life. You may have a picture of how you want your life to turn out, but some things are out of your control. The people on the planes and in the World Trade Center didn't plan for their lives to end on September 11, 2001. Their families didn't plan on it either. Sadly, they didn't reach their final destinations in life. Stuff happens. But having a goal for your life gives you a better chance of getting there while you're alive.

When I talk about dreams, I'm not talking about the ones you have when you are sleeping. I mean things that you want to accomplish in life. Dreams are things you want to do with your life. They are an important part of who you are. Someone once said, "The vision that you glory in your mind, the ideal that you enthrone in your heart– this you will build your life by, this will you become." The vision and ideal that it's talking about are other ways to say goals and dreams. The dreams you follow help you become the person you want to be. They guide you on your success journey.

Goals are stops along the way to your dreams. You put a date with a goal. You say, "I will do this by that time." Small goals get you closer to big goals. Big goals move you closer to your bigger goals. Reaching your bigger goals sends you toward your biggest goals and dreams.

These goals are the compass. They tell which direction to go to get to the destination–your dreams. They let you know if you are traveling in the right direction. If you aren't, they can point you back in the right direction. A compass always points north. Your goals point to your dreams. Learn to use goals as a compass and map to your most important possessions–your dreams!

ॐ

"The dreams you see most clearly are the ones most likely to come true." –Barney

Okay, I know you are ready to put down the book now because there is a quote from Barney. Hang on a second and give me a chance to explain. Believe me, I can't stand him either, but my daughter likes watching the *Barney Movie*. She was watching it one day and I heard him say this.

The movie is about three kids and Barney chasing an egg that fell from space. They discover that it is a dream catcher. They finally get it and return it to the spot where they found it. The egg hatches and a little furry guy comes out. He is the dream catcher. All of a sudden there is a scene of one of the girls on a horse winning a horse race. She says, "I've never seen it [her dream] so clearly before." Then Barney replies, "The dreams you see most clearly are the ones most likely to come true."

I know it's Barney and all, but what he says is so true. Dreams and goals are targets. The targets you see most clearly are the ones you are most likely to hit. If you aren't aiming at anything, then you could hit nothing.

Tara Lipinski was an Olympic gold medal figure skater. She was five years old during the 1988 Winter Olympics. She watched the figure skating finals. The night that the gold medal was given to Katarina Witt, Tara walked up on boxes in her living room and received an imaginary gold medal from her father. Ten years later to the day, she walked up and received a real gold medal at the 1998 Winter Olympics. She pictured that victory clearly in her mind ten years earlier.

What do coaches say when they are teaching someone to hit a baseball or golf ball? "Keep your eye on the ball." The ball is the target you are trying to hit. If you take your eye off the ball, you may end up hitting nothing. Keep your eye on your dreams. It greatly increases your chances of hitting them!

"Where there is passion and desire, there will always be a new frontier."

"Space, the final frontier." That's the way the original Star Trek used to start. For those who like adventure there are always new frontiers. A frontier is past the edge of what we already know and have experienced. In the early 1800s, the Mississippi River marked the edge of what was known about this continent to the Americans. Beyond the Mississippi lay the new frontier. New land. New adventures. New experiences. New dangers.

Explorers moved west to find out what was there. New frontiers always bring new opportunities. Gold was discovered out west. Good land was discovered.

In the late 1950s and 1960s the new frontier was space. The Soviet Union sent the first object into space to orbit the earth. It was a little satellite that sent beeps back to earth. It did nothing else. That opened the new frontier in space. The United States, who was an enemy of the Soviet Union, raced to beat them into space. The Soviets won again when Yuri Gagarin was the first human to ever go into space.

The U.S. and Soviet Union kept trying to outdo the other. It was the U.S. that won the ultimate prize. On July 20, 1969,

Neil Armstrong became the first human ever to step out onto ground of something other than the earth. It was "one small step for man, one giant leap for mankind," he said as he set foot on the moon.

What got man to the moon? It was passion and desire. The men who risked their lives to travel 240,000 miles to the moon and 240,000 miles back had to have a passion for it. It was more important to them than the chance of dying.

The men who designed the rocket had a passion for this project. Their ideas would carry men to the moon. Wherner Von Braun, the chief designer of the gigantic Saturn V rocket, dreamed of doing that since he was a kid. The people in Mission Control had a passion for their work. It was something that was very important to them. Their skill would return the men to earth safely. The whole nation had a passion for the project. It would show the world who was the best.

A passion is a desire that makes your heart beat faster when you think about it. You smile a lot when you are thinking about or talking about your passion. It is something that is a part of you. It is part of what makes YOU.

I've said before that I want to race cars. That is a passion for me. When I think about it, I get a huge smile. Once I start talking about it, you can't get me to shut up. There is something inside me that glows red hot when that topic comes up. I feel like a kid at Christmas when they see all the presents for them! Racing is a desire in my heart that is a part of me. If I try to act like it isn't important, I would be lying to myself. Anyone who knows me well, knows this desire about me. My third grade students know this.

What is it for you? What is important to you that makes you glow red hot when you think or talk about it? That is your passion. You may not be able to tell yet. That's okay. You're young. You've got time. Just keep your eyes open. Look for those things that you enjoy doing. That could be a clue.

A new frontier filled with excitement and opportunity awaits you on the other side of your desires and passions. When you figure out what they are, life truly begins!

"Nothing happens unless first a dream."

I have always wanted to write a book. I look at some of the books for babies, you know the ones with a word on each page, and think, "Why don't I write a story." If people will buy those things, I should be able to write something. I even tried a few times. I have a few half-finished stories somewhere around my house.

I always dreamed of writing a book. I knew I had a story inside me somewhere. Without that dream, you wouldn't be reading this now. Nothing worthwhile happens if someone doesn't have a dream to do it.

Do you think Thomas Edison had a dream of an electric light? He must have, to keep trying thousands of times to get it to work. The same can be said for the Wright brothers and the men who designed and flew the first spaceships.

Christopher Columbus had a dream. He waited for about six years before he was able to get King Ferdinand and Queen Isabela of Spain to pay for his trip. Not only did he wait that long, but he wanted to take a trip that most people thought would kill him. See, he wanted to sail AROUND the world. Most people thought it was flat. They thought that you would come to the end of the world and just fall off the edge into space.

He believed that the earth was like a ball. He wanted to get to the East Indies, islands off the coast of Asia. To get there by boat, you had to sail to the south of Africa and then into the Indian Ocean to the East Indies. The other way to get there was to take a long trip over land. By long I mean that it would take a few years to get there and back. Columbus dreamed of getting there by sailing the opposite way and coming to them from the other side. He believed in his dream so strongly that he was willing to die to prove that it could be done.

Did he get to the East Indies on his trip? No. He bumped into Puerto Rico, Cuba, and the other islands off the southeast coast of the United States. Of course it wasn't called the United

States then. No "white" people lived there yet. The Native Americans were the only ones living there.

He dreamed of going all the way around the world to get to the East Indies. Little did he know that there were two other continents in the way! He ended up discovering that the world was like a ball and that there was a "New World" waiting to be explored.

Keep looking for your dreams. They will come to you as you grow. Where might your dreams someday lead you? Where might your dreams someday lead all of us?

"There in the sunshine are my highest aspirations. I may not reach them, but I can look up and see their beauty, believe in them, and try to follow where they lead."

Your dreams are beautiful things. When you truly find a dream, it brings life to you. Dreams give your life a purpose. I've heard it said that you should never get in the way of someone who is pursuing a dream. They will run you over.

Of course, if your dream is to be a professional athlete or President or something like that, there is a good chance that you may never get there. But if that is truly your dream, you have to run after it. Remember that your dream doesn't have to be something as grand as one of those. I dream of making a difference in kids' lives. That's why I became a teacher. Whatever makes you feel important and good about yourself can be your dream.

The quote uses the word "aspirations." It means the same as dreams and goals. It comes from the word "aspire." It means to reach for something that you really want. Keep your aspirations in front of you. They will be a guide to you. They will lead you to a great destination. Your goals and dreams, your aspirations, will be the fuel for you as you travel on the success journey.

It must be sad to look into the eyes of someone who is about to die that didn't try to follow their dreams. They look back on their life and are full of regret. They know that they missed their opportunity. Regret is when you are sad for the things that you did, or didn't do. Don't be in the position of coming to the end of your life and feeling that you wasted it. That is the saddest way to die.

Keep your dreams in front of you and never let someone else steal them! They are like gold to you. That's how valuable they are. Protect them and take care of them. They will give you joy in life as you follow them!

"Personality doesn't make a person extraordinary; neither does intelligence or education. What makes a person extraordinary is purpose–the consuming desire to accomplish something in life."

Extraordinary. It is a funny word. It looks like a compound word made up of the words *extra* and *ordinary*, but that's not what it is. Let me explain.

Ordinary is a word that describes how many people in the world choose to live their lives. Ordinary means that there is nothing special about something. It is like all the rest. There is nothing unique about it.

I said that ordinary is how some people *choose* to live their lives, but there are no ordinary people. Everyone is special and unique! Everyone has a special purpose on this earth! You are no mistake. No one is.

Negative messages bombard you all day, every day. The messages attack the feeling that you are unique and special. How many times have you heard a message, even coming from your own mind, that says you are dumb or a failure or can't do anything right? You aren't wearing the right clothes or shoes. Life is hopeless. You live and then die. There is nothing left after someone dies. Your ancestors were monkeys and apes that changed into humans. You are too skinny or too fat. You messed up again. You'll never get it right. Do it; everyone else is. Chicken. Don't get your hopes up; you'll only get disappointed.

When was the last time you heard that you are a winner! You can do anything you set your mind to. You messed up, but you'll get it next time. Nice try! Life is a great adventure. I love you the way you are. There is more than just this life. God made you special and has a plan for you! I'm proud of you. Don't give up; I believe in you. Dream big dreams! Shoot for your dreams!

We aren't ordinary. Unfortunately some people can't believe they are special so they live an ordinary life. I said that *extraordinary* is a funny word. If it were a compound word it would mean that something is extra ordinary, or more ordinary. However, *extra* is a prefix that means *beyond*. When something is extraordinary it is way beyond ordinary. It is so much better than something that is ordinary.

What makes a person extraordinary? It isn't personality. People can be successful if they are outgoing and friendly or shy. A person can have a dream if they are assertive, or tell people what they want, or if they are less demanding. People can set goals if they are serious or funny. It doesn't matter what your personality is. You can still be successful.

The quote also says that it isn't intelligence or education. Remember Orville and Wilbur Wright? They were just bicycle repairmen. They owned a bike repair shop in Ohio. They never went to college. Samuel P. Langley, the other man trying to make the plane carry a person, was a college professor. He had all the education. The Wright brothers had all the desire to accomplish something. Had you ever heard of Langley before reading this book? I hadn't heard of him either until I read it in another book. Who was more extraordinary?

The extraordinary people are the ones who still dream. They see that there is a purpose, or plan, for their lives. They go way beyond ordinary people and have a strong desire to do something with their lives. Anyone can be extraordinary. Do you dare to dream and chase that dream? You can be extraordinary too.

"The tragedy of life is what dies inside a man while he lives." –Albert Schwietzer

The movie *Braveheart* is about a man named William Wallace who lived in Scotland in the 1600s. At that time Scotland was part of the British Empire. That means that King Edward of England was also the King of Scotland. William

Wallace wanted to be free. That was his dream. He didn't want an English king; he wanted a Scottish one.

He led many of the Scottish farmers in a revolt against the king. He led the Scottish to a major victory over the highly trained English army. He was a hero in Scotland. He was an outlaw in England.

Eventually he got captured and was sentenced to death. While in the dungeon, the princess visited him. He told her that "every man dies, but not every man really lives." What does that mean? The quote explains it.

The saddest thing in life is when your dreams die. There is no purpose for living after that. How do dreams die? The pressures of life overwhelm a person so that she can no longer dream of doing what she always wanted. She has to be realistic and get a good job to help pay the bills. He has to take a job he hates because the family needs the money. Each day that passes strangles the dream a little more. Soon it dies a horrible death. You've seen people like that. There is no sparkle in their eyes or joy on their faces. Don't let yourself die while you're still alive!

Your dreams are a God-given part of you that makes you special. They give you life! Keep them in front of you so that you are really alive. The best way to remember your dreams is to have pictures on your wall of things that represent them. What you picture becomes real to your mind. Keep real pictures in front of you often to remind you. Also, act like you have already achieved your goals. By acting that way you will start to see yourself that way. Seeing yourself like that makes you work toward it even more. It actually helps your dreams and goals come true.

George Herbert said, "He begins to die, that quits his desires." Don't let your dreams die inside you while you're still alive! Keep your dreams out in the fresh air and light so they will live. When they live, you really live. Be a dream chaser!

"One can never consent to creep when one feels the impulse to soar." — Helen Keller

Here is another great quote from Helen Keller. Remember

that she was blind and deaf? She is telling us that if you have dreams inside you, you must follow them. You won't be happy if you don't.

An eagle is a majestic bird. It loves to soar on the winds. It would never be happy walking around on the ground. It wasn't made to walk. It was made to fly high and free on the winds!

The same is true for people. We weren't made to live little lives creeping around on the ground, going to work 8-10 hours a day, 5-6 days a week for 50 weeks a year for 40 years. Adults are usually so tired from the routine that they have little energy left to play with their kids. You think going to school is no fun. Most adults think work is no fun. Their time and lives are not really their own. This creeping around isn't what we were made for. We were made to live free and soar to great heights with our lives!

How do you soar with your life? Follow your dreams. Extraordinary people are the ones with a burning desire to do something with their lives. Gil Bailie is an author. He wrote, "Don't ask yourself what the world needs. Ask yourself what makes you come alive, and go do that, because what the world needs is people who have come alive." There are too many people creeping on this earth. We need people who have come alive to spark something in others that may help them to find their dreams again and come alive. Be one of the alive people!

Helen Keller wanted to soar. When Annie met Helen she could see that Helen had a spirit in her that couldn't be held down by blindness or deafness. The day at the water pump was the day that Helen got her wings. After that, Annie taught Helen to soar. Helen went on to college and graduated with good grades. She wrote books and gave speeches. She made a difference with her life. She lived more than many people who can see and hear.

Let your dreams make you alive. Don't be satisfied with a life of creeping. Spread your wings, and let your dreams carry you high into the sky to fly free!

Chapter 5

Your Future and Destiny

What do you want to be when you grow up? You may have thought about it before. You may not have. It isn't too early to think about it. Remember that goals and dreams are like targets. If you have something you are aiming at, you have a better chance of hitting it.

Each day you are either moving closer to your goals, standing still, or moving away from your goals. I want to race cars. I didn't do anything to move myself toward that goal early in life. Space and the Apollo missions to the moon also fascinated me. However, I never set goals and moved toward that. That's why I'm not a racecar driver or an astronaut at this time. Now it is too late for me to achieve those goals. I am trying to get into Karts. They are faster than the go-karts at the amusement park. They are really little racecars. I'll never be a professional driver at this stage, but I can still satisfy that dream in some way.

If you start finding your dreams now, you will be able to start moving in that direction now. The sooner you start, the closer you'll be when opportunities arise. You'll also be able to create chances to achieve those goals when you know where you are going.

You were created to live a life that makes a difference. You were created to live a life of adventure. You were created to soar, like Helen Keller said.

The people who live great lives, the people who soar, don't

wait for things to happen to them and then react to it. People who soar make things happen in their lives. They create the life they want. Too many people are letting their bosses make a life for them. The boss tells them when they get up, start work, eat lunch, go home, when they take a vacation, when the vacation is over, what kind of vacation because of how much money they make, and the list goes on.

You can never control everything in your life. There are always things that happen that you can't control. But if you have a plan for your life, you can at least control the direction you are traveling. You can put yourself on a path toward something. You put yourself in a position to take advantage of opportunities by traveling in a definite direction. You know where you are going and can look at situations and take advantage of the ones that will help you get to where you want to go. The people who don't have a destination in mind can't do that. They have no destination, so they don't know if the opportunity will be good for them or not.

"The best way to predict the future is to create it."

Have you seen TV shows where someone goes to the lady with the crystal ball to tell them the future? Or maybe you've seen the commercials where you can call in and the person will tell you your future based on some cards. Wouldn't it be nice to know the future? Wouldn't it be nice to know which opportunities would turn out fine and which ones wouldn't work out too well? Maybe, maybe not.

There is no way to know the future for sure. Get over it. The best way there is to know the future is to go out and put yourself in a position to make things happen to move you toward your goals. George Bernard Shaw said the same thing this way, "The people who get on in this world are the people who get up and look for the circumstances they want, and, if they can't find them, make them."

Successful people are always working to reach their goals and dreams. They are *proactive*. In other words, they work to *make* things happen. They get up and put themselves in positions to take advantage of things that come along. Unsuccessful people react to things that happen. That means that things happen and then they act depending on what happened. Usually it is too late to take advantage of the opportunity at that point.

When you make things happen, you have a little more control over what happens to you. That makes sense, doesn't it? For example, when you know a test is coming you can study for it. That puts you in more control of the grade you get on the test. You made the grade happen because you put yourself in position by studying.

Some people react to things. They don't go out and make it happen. That's like when you have a pop quiz. The teacher made it happen and you didn't expect it. Now you have to react to the quiz and give the answers. The teacher has more of the control over the grade. You are reacting to the quiz. Now, if you are prepared and read the lesson then you would have a little more control over your grade.

Don't be a reactor. Make your life happen. Don't let life happen to you. Go out and put yourself into a position to make opportunities happen that will move you toward your goals and dreams. Make the situations and opportunities happen that will move you along on the success journey.

"The only limit to our realization of tomorrow will be our doubts of today."
–Franklin D. Roosevelt

A lot of people miss opportunities because they doubt that they can succeed. The quote says that the only things that keep us from succeeding in the future are the doubts we have today. I said before that I have always wanted to write a book. I just didn't think I could do it. I love good stories, and they make me want to write a great story. Every time I started, it ended up sounding like the story I just read. I doubted I could do it. I never finished the story because I thought that no one but me would want to read it. I limited myself by doubting myself.

I've talked to many people who look at their abilities right now and don't attempt something new because they doubt they can do it. They forget that they can learn and grow to do it. Think about yourself now and in the past. You have learned to write cursive, do multiplication, division, and all kinds of other things in the last year. Think of all the things you've learned to do that you couldn't do last year. Learning never ends unless you choose to stop learning.

Maybe you know someone in your class or school who doesn't like to read much. They aren't doing well in school because of it. Do other kids tease or make fun of that kid? I hope you don't. There are many reasons why kids have trouble in school. The point is that many adults, parents or teachers, call that kid "slow" or "not motivated." When an adult with a job, a family, and bills to pay doesn't read or grow anymore, other adults call him "normal." The other adults have stopped reading and growing too, so it is normal behavior for most adults.

The way to be successful in life is to read and learn and grow each day. If that is a habit for you, you will be able to take advantage of the opportunities that come your way. You won't doubt your ability to do it because you know that you can learn and grow to do it. Will you always succeed the first time? Of course not! But if you fail the first time, you know that you can learn from the failure and try again with a better chance to succeed.

Don't fear trying and failing. President Roosevelt also said, "that the only thing we have to fear is fear itself." He meant that fear would keep you from trying. There is no need to fear failure. Is there something you haven't tried lately because you doubted you could do it? Learning to do this would be like all the other things you have learned. Give it a try. Don't let your doubts limit your future. Think of all the things you've learned in the last year. The worst that could happen is that you could fail and learn a lesson from it. The best that could happen is that you could succeed and feel great about yourself!

"The future belongs to those who believe in the beauty of their dreams." — Eleanor Roosevelt

Here we are back to the goals and dreams stuff again. Is it really that important? Yes it is! Like I've said before, when you have a dream, you come alive. The world needs people who are alive. Let's look at the life of many adults and see if this is what you hope your future will be like.

The alarm goes off at 5:30 a.m. to get you up for work. Your spouse, husband or wife, gets up then too. You both have to work to pay all the bills. You rush through the shower and get dressed. You grab a piece of toast as you run out the door to head to work, while your spouse gets the kids ready. You drive for an hour or more in traffic to get to work by 8:30. Your spouse gets the kids to daycare and is at work by 9:00.

You work all day: answering phone calls, making phone calls, writing reports for the boss, going to meetings and so on. Or maybe you don't work in an office. Maybe you work in another field where you are lifting, carrying, moving, and sweating all day. Either way, you get a lunch break. Well, maybe you need to get caught up on some things, so you eat at your desk or on the run and keep working.

You get a few other breaks during the day, but they don't help. You leave work at 5:00 tired as a dog. You now drive home for an hour in traffic to get the kids from day care. You get home at 6:15. Now you or your spouse has to eat quickly because your son has baseball practice at 6:45. Your daughter has softball practice at 7:00, but luckily it isn't your day to drive the car pool.

When you all get back together at 8:00, your son says that he has homework that he didn't finish at day care. It is something that should have been done, but he was messing around instead of doing it. You are frustrated with him. Now he will be up until 9:30 doing it. You and he fight about it the whole time because he still doesn't just get to it and finish.

He finally goes to bed, but you are mad at each other. You collapse in front of the TV with your spouse and watch two shows. It is now 10:30. You start getting ready for bed. You haven't had much time to really talk to your spouse; both of you were just watching the TV and not talking. As you are getting ready for bed, one of you mentions that the car wasn't running right. You think that the brakes are bad and figure that it will cost about $500.

At 11:00 you drag yourself into bed wondering where you will get the money to fix the car. As you drift off to sleep you hear the alarm going off to get you up to start all over again. And how long does this last for the average person? Fifty weeks a year for forty years. How does that sound? Do you see why MOST adults are not really happy with their lives? Is that really living?

Someone once said, "When there is hope in the future there is power in the present." That means that when you have a hope for a better future, you have power to do things NOW. You have more energy to do things because the things you are doing are getting you closer to your goals and dreams.

I am a teacher. I am doing something else after my teaching day is over to create some more money and choices in my life. A few years ago, I was very unhappy with life. I felt trapped because I knew that the money I made as a teacher was barely enough to pay the bills each month. There were no nice vacations each summer. There was never enough money to go out with my wife. I had no hope. I didn't know what I was going to do.

Since I felt trapped, I had a bad attitude at school. I wasn't patient with my students. I was pretty mean. I couldn't wait to get out of there each day. It doesn't sound like a nice classroom to be in, does it? It wasn't. Then a friend showed me a way to make extra money. I was ready to listen. What he showed me was a way to have the extra money to go on a nice vacation or out with my wife. It gave me HOPE!

I could dare to dream of having a kart to race. My dreams came alive again. I came alive again! I had power now to do the things I needed to do. I started learning about success, failure, dreams and everything else in this book. I started dreaming about writing a book, because I believed in myself and wasn't afraid to fail. This was the idea that I came up with. The future is now mine! I can make it happen and that hope gives me POWER!

"In times of change there is no incentive so great, and no medicine so powerful as hope for a better tomorrow."

Do you remember the book *Charlie and the Chocolate Factory* or the movie *Willy Wonka and the Chocolate Factory*? If you haven't read it or seen the movie, I highly recommend them. It is a story about a poor boy and his family. Charlie has a lot of character. He is kind, helpful, and honest.

Willy Wonka owns the most famous chocolate factory in the world. He makes the most delicious and interesting candies. He hides five golden tickets in five candy bars. The people who find a ticket will get the chance to visit the factory and win a lifetime supply of chocolate! There is a mad rush to buy Wonka Bars. Charlie, however, is so poor that he only gets one bar of chocolate a year on his birthday.

Charlie had a rough life. He has no father in the movie. There are four old grandparents, Charlie's mom, and Charlie living in an old shack. One time Charlie brings home a large loaf of bread and the family is excited because they will get more to eat. When was the last time you were excited when your mom brought home a loaf of bread?

When he is about to open the bar of chocolate that he got for his birthday he says, "I've got the same chance as anyone else." His Grandpa Joe replies, "You've got more, Charlie, because you want it more." Charlie wanted to believe that it was possible that he could find a ticket with only one candy bar. He didn't really have a good chance, but he had hope. That hope was what kept him going. Since he is the hero of the story, of course, he eventually finds one of the tickets.

He finds some money in the street and buys a Wonka bar. The last Golden Ticket is in there and he runs home to tell his family. Grandpa Joe is as excited as Charlie. He actually gets out of bed. He says that he hasn't done that in twenty years. Then he and Charlie sing a song. It is a great song about the power of hope. Look at the words to the song:

I never thought my life could be anything but catastrophe, but suddenly I begin to see a bit of good luck for me. 'Cause I've got a golden ticket. I've got a golden twinkle in my eye.

I never had a chance to shine, never a happy song to sing, but suddenly half the world is mine. What an amazing thing 'cause I've got a golden ticket. I've got a golden sun up in the sky.

I never thought I'd see the day when I would face the world and say, "Good morning. Look at the sun."

I never thought I would be slap in the lap of luxury 'cause I'd have said it couldn't be done. But it can be done!

I never dreamed that I would climb over the moon in ecstasy but never the less it's there that I'm shortly about to be 'cause I've got a golden ticket. I've got a golden chance to make my way, and with a golden ticket it's a golden day.

Do you see the words of hope in the song? He has a golden ticket that gives him hope of a better tomorrow. His golden ticket makes this a golden day. Have you ever had a golden day? That is one when everything goes right. Think of the first day of summer vacation–that is a golden day!

When my friend showed me a way to make some extra money to make it possible for me to take my wife out and take a vacation with my family, he gave me a golden ticket. With that golden ticket, I had a golden chance to make my way. He didn't give me money. He didn't hand me anything. He gave me a chance to do it myself. Now each day is a golden day because I have hope.

Do you remember a time when there were several days of rainy or snowy or cloudy weather? The sun didn't shine for those days. Then the next day comes and the sun is out shining brightly. You feel a lot better when the sun is shining. In parts of

Alaska the sun doesn't shine for several months each year. The northern hemisphere is tilted away from the sun, so it doesn't get sunlight. The people that live in those regions get more depressed, or sad, at that time of the year. When the sun comes back in early spring, the people feel much better.

Hope is like that too. When things look bad, the sun has set and doesn't rise. It is always dark and people get depressed. When something gives hope, the light blasts into the darkness and the sun rises. Then people aren't as sad. It becomes a golden day.

Find your own golden ticket. Find what gives you hope for a better tomorrow. You must search for your golden ticket just like the people in the movie searched for the golden tickets. Don't ever stop searching until you find one; then each day will be golden!

"Destiny is not a matter of chance, it is a matter of choice; it is not a thing to be waited for, it is a thing to be achieved." —William Jennings Bryan

Do you know that the chance of winning the lottery is almost the same if you have one ticket or no ticket? Yet people will go buy a ticket every week to have that teeny tiny chance of winning millions of dollars. They put their hopes for a better future on that teeny tiny chance of striking it rich.

Your future isn't something to place bets on. It isn't something to leave up to chance. Remember playing pin the tail on the donkey at birthday parties? Many people go through life like they are playing that. They are blindfolded because they have no goals or dreams. They get spun around by life until they don't know which way to go. They have to get up, work, come home exhausted, try to be good parents, and collapse into bed still worried about where the money to pay all the bills will come from. They become dizzy and disoriented. Then they try to find one spot that will make them win. They have no way to see where they are going and are dizzy. They walk around trying to pin their hopes of winning in the right spot. That is not a good way to look at your future.

People who succeed don't wait for things to happen to them. Successful people go out and look for opportunities. People who don't succeed wait for everything to be perfect before they act on an opportunity. The problem is that it never happens. While one thing works out, other things go bad. There is a story of two shoe salesmen who went to the same area in the South to sell shoes to the people who lived there. They were both eager to make big sales. It was the summer, and they noticed that everyone just went barefoot while working around the farms. One of the salesmen called back to the office and asked to be transferred. He said, "I want to sell in another place. None of these people wear shoes." The other salesman called back to the office and said, "Send me five more crates of shoes. None of these people wear shoes!"

Do you see what happened? They saw the same situation. One saw a problem: " None of these people wear shoes." The other saw an opportunity: " None of these people wear shoes!" Your destiny is not something you wait for until everything is perfect. Your destiny is for you to go out and make the most of every thing that happens to you.

Your future is your choice. Your goals and dreams guide you. They give you hope so you don't get dizzy and disoriented. You can see where you are headed. You know what you are pinning your hopes on. You have a clear direction to go with your time and money. Everything you do has a purpose, and that purpose it to reach your goals and dreams.

A friend once said to me, "If it is to be, it is up to me." Wow! Those ten, two letter words say it better than a whole book could say it. It is up to you to make your life meaningful. It is up to you to do something special with your life. It is up to you!

Chapter 6

Belief

Y「ou have probably realized by now that all the things we have explored are connected. Your dreams and goals give you hope for the future. How you react to failure as you try to accomplish your goals affects your attitude. When you have a good attitude you look on failure as a lesson. Your attitude makes you enjoy the success journey.

Now I will throw another characteristic in that also affects the others–belief. You must believe in yourself, the goodness of your dream, and your ability to look any situation in the face and say, "You will not beat me." You must believe that your attitude is a powerful weapon to fight the negative influences of the world. You must believe that your future has great things for you if you follow your dreams. You must believe that failure can't stop you. You must believe.

Let me tell you a story that shows what belief really means. There was a high wire walker who stretched a wire across Niagara falls. He used a wheel barrow filled with 200 pounds of rocks as his balancing aid.

A large crowd gathered to watch him attempt to walk across Niagara Falls pushing the wheel barrow. There were many reporters there to cover the story. They all watched amazed as he got on the wire and pushed the 200 pound load across!

The people and reporters went crazy when he got to the other side. The reporters were all asking questions for their stories. There was one reporter that seemed very interested and was asking a lot of questions. The tight rope walker asked the reporter, "Do you THINK I can do it again?" The reporter replied, "Yes, I THINK you can do it again." The tight rope walker asked him again, "Do you BELIEVE I can do it again?" The reporter was a little confused. He answered, "Yes, I BELIEVE you can do it again." The walker dumped the rocks out of the wheel barrow and said, "Get in."

There is a difference in saying you believe and really believing. The reporter was amazed by what he saw. He said that he believed that it could be done again. When he was asked to put action to that belief, he showed that he didn't really believe. You see, he didn't get in the wheel barrow. True belief will show up as action.

When you truly believe in yourself you will act in ways that show it. You will try things that may seem hard. You will not be afraid to fail. You will be positive about yourself and not say negative things about yourself. You won't believe the lies that others say about you either.

⚬⤷

"You must first be a believer if you would be an achiever."

"I think I can. I think I can. I think I can." Do you remember what story that is from? It is from *The Little Engine That Could*. The train that was carrying all the toys and goodies to the other side of the mountain broke down. Other trains came by, but they felt that they were too good and important to pull a toy train, None of them helped.

Then came along the Little Engine. His job was to hook up the cars to the other engines at the train yards. He was small because he was used to pulling one or two cars at a time. He saw that the toys were sad because they couldn't get over the mountain to the good little boys and girls. He decided to try and help. He hooked up and started up the mountain.

The little engine chugged away, pulling the cars slowly up the mountain. As it got tough to pull he started believing in himself. He started chanting, "I think I can. I think I can. I think

I can." He finally reached the top of the mountain and started the easy trip down. As he picked up speed, he started saying, "I thought I could! I thought I could! I thought I could!"

He believed in his power and he was able to succeed at the task. It's the same way with us. I had a student tell me that he couldn't do well on the science test. It was a test on plants and how they grow. Only a few weeks earlier he had gotten an "*A*" on a social studies test on the parts of our country's government and what they do. That is harder than remembering what stems, roots, and leaves do. Don't you agree?

He said that he got a bad grade "because I can't do plants." Of course you can't if you say you can't! Do you remember what Henry Ford said about belief? "Whether you think you can, or think you can't...you're right." This student told himself that he couldn't and he didn't. I tried to show him that if he could learn the branches of government, he could learn what plant parts do. There is no difference. It doesn't matter what the topic is. You have learned a lot in the past. That shows you that you can do it. You have done it in the past, so you can do it again now and in the future.

You cannot succeed at anything if you don't believe that you can. Belief is the first step. The next few pages will tell about the things you have to believe in to succeed. Probably the most important thing to believe in the gifts that God has given you. The Greek philosopher and poet Virgil said, "They can who believe they can." It starts with belief in yourself.

"As a man thinks in his heart, so he is."
–King Solomon

Abraham Lincoln was maybe the greatest President this country has ever seen. He led the nation through a very hard time in our history. He kept this nation together. If it wasn't for his leadership, this land we call the United States of America could have been two or more separate countries.

Throughout the founding of our country and in 1787 when the Constitution was written, many people in America owned slaves. Slaves were people that worked for their masters. They didn't get paid like regular workers. The master owned the slave like a piece of property. It wasn't right or fair. That's just the way it was. The 1770 Census, a count of all the people in a country, records that there were 59,196 free people living in America and 694,204 slaves. That means that the average person owned about 12 slaves. By 1860 there were almost 4 million slaves in America!

Most of the people that lived in the northern part of the country didn't own slaves. Most of the people that lived in the southern part of the country did own slaves. There were many cotton farms, or plantations, in the South. Slaves were used to do all the work on the plantations. The plantation owners would go to the city when new slaves were brought in from Africa and buy some of them. Then the slaves, the people, would belong to the plantation owner. Like I said, it wasn't right or fair. That's just the way it was.

A lot of people in the North didn't like the idea of one person owning another person. There were stories of cruel slave owners that beat slaves with whips to punish them. The government wanted to pass laws that would make it illegal to own slaves. The people in the South didn't like that idea. The leaders of the southern states decided that they would not be part of the country anymore. They would secede from the Union. Abraham Lincoln wasn't going to let that happen.

That's when the Civil War started. A civil war is where the people of a country fight against themselves. It isn't one country against another; it is citizens of the same country fighting. The South wanted to be free to own slaves. The North didn't think that was right. Lincoln didn't think they had the right to just quit being part of the country because they didn't like some of the decisions. For five years the country was at war.

Eventually the North won the war. The South wasn't going to secede from the country. Abraham Lincoln freed the slaves. This didn't make everyone happy. There were Southerners who didn't like Lincoln. He started to rebuild the country after the terrible war.

One evening he went to Ford's Theater in Washington,

D.C. to watch a play. While he was there, a man named John Wilkes Booth shot him in the back of the head. Booth didn't like the things that Lincoln had done. The greatest president was dead.

What does that have to do with the quote? The quote says, "As a man thinks in his heart, so he is." In other words, whatever you think about yourself is what you will be. "If you think you can, you're right. If you think you can't, you're right about that too." If you think you are a loser, then you are a loser. That will set you up in a negative cycle that will make you act like a loser and lead to failures. If you think you're a winner, then you will act like a winner and start a positive chain reaction that will help you succeed.

What did Lincoln think about himself during this time? Did he think he was a winner or a loser? Not everyone thought he was a great man at that time. Many people, especially in the South, hated him. The night he was shot, April 14, 1865, gives us some clues to what he thought about himself. When he was shot he had five things in his pockets: a handkerchief, his glasses, a pocket knife, $5 in Confederate money, and a newspaper clipping. Confederate money was the money that the Confederacy, the southern states that tried to secede, printed during the war.

The newspaper article quoted British statesman John Bright. He said, "Abraham Lincoln is the greatest leader of men." Lincoln must have had doubts that what he did was the right thing. Many people hated him. He must have felt pretty low at times. When he did, he must have pulled that article out and read those words that gave him the courage to go on. "Abraham Lincoln is the greatest leader of men." That made him feel like a winner again so he could go on with the tough job of reuniting the country and healing the wounds after the war. Unfortunately, a coward's bullet took his life before his work was done.

What do you think about yourself? It is important to know. Those thoughts control much of what you do and the attitudes that you have. That is why it is important to fill your mind with positive input. The negative input that hits you from every side is enough to kill your good thoughts of yourself. The positive input is the only way to defend yourself. Do something every day to fill your mind with positive thoughts. Don't let someone else's wrong opinion of you affect your thinking. You are great. You can do whatever you want to in life. You have strengths and abilities that will take you far if you use them!

"Nothing in this world is impossible to a willing heart."

Think of all the things that have happened in this world that people once said were impossible. Hold on, this is going to be a fast ride of facts and figures.

People once thought that if you sailed too far you would fall off the earth. You would just go off into space. It took someone with a willing heart to try and sail west to get to the east to prove them wrong. Now we all know about an Italian sailor named Christopher Columbus.

In most McDonald's restaurants is a plaque telling the story of the founder, Ray Kroc. You may be wondering why it's called McDonald's. Ray Kroc was a milkshake machine salesman. He was in California selling his machines to the McDonald brothers. They owned two restaurants that served hamburgers, fried potatoes, and shakes for people on the go. Ray Kroc saw that they had a great idea. He told them of a plan to open more McDonald's restaurants in other parts of the country. They told him that it was impossible. At that time, most people ate at home. There was a limited demand for food on the go. They sold him the restaurants and the name for between one and two million dollars. They thought he was a fool! Now there are McDonald's restaurants in most countries around the world. His willing heart started a huge chain of restaurants that have served close to 100 billion hamburgers. That's enough hamburgers to go around the earth almost 379 times!

A lot of people that showed up to see Samuel Langley's plane try to fly were there to make fun of him. When he failed both times they used that as proof that it was impossible to make a plane that had an engine to carry people. However, a few days later the willing hearts of the Wright brothers proved that it could be done. Then people thought it was impossible to make planes that carried more than a few people at a time. Look at the huge jets that carry hundreds of people. There are military jets that can fly faster than the speed of sound. They can reach speeds close to 3,000 miles an hour!

The first races in America were in the 1890s. The speeds of the cars didn't impress most people. There are movies that show people running faster than the cars! Most people thought it was cool that there was a carriage that didn't have a horse pulling it. It was new and fun to see. Few people thought that they would ever be useful. Henry Ford had other ideas and a willing heart. He improved his designs and made them cheaper. The number of cars the Ford Motor company made each year went from 10,000 in 1911 to about 250,000 a year in 1914. This was his third company. The other two went out of business. What about the speeds of cars now? The record for the fastest racecar on a racetrack is held by Gil DeFeran at over 240 miles an hour!

I am writing this with a computer sitting on my lap. The first computers in the 1940s were the size of whole rooms! Some people thought that because they were so big there wouldn't be a need for too many computers. The president of IBM once said that there was only a market for about five computers in the whole world. Boy, was he wrong. Two men with willing hearts, Steve Jobs and Steve Wozniak, built a circuit board for a computer in the late 1970s. They took it to the company they worked for and told them of their idea to make a computer for the average people. Atari, the company they worked for, turned them down. They didn't think that people would want a complicated computer. They found a few people to give them money to start making some of these computers. They used the money to start Apple Computer in Steve Jobs' parent's garage.

People dreamed about walking on the moon a long time ago. Jules Verne wrote a book called *From the Earth to the Moon* in the 1865. It was a great success. People loved the book but thought it was impossible to go to the moon. Remember, there weren't even airplanes yet. A hundred years later Neil Armstrong set foot on the moon for the first time. All of the people who worked to get men to the moon had willing hearts.

The first cell phones had cords attached to bags that you had to carry. People thought that it was impossible. Now look at the size of some cell phones. They are small enough that you could hide one in your hand. Nothing is impossible.

George Bernard Shaw said, "You see things; and you say, 'Why?' But I dream things that never were; and I say, 'Why not?'" People who invent things or come up with new ideas are dreamers. Most people have forgotten how to dream though. Most people are limited by what they see. They see difficulties in something new and ask why they need to change. Dreamers, the people who come up with new ideas and ways of doing things, look at the same situation and see the chance to change something to make it better. Someone else said "Those who say it can't be done are usually interrupted by others doing it." The ones doing it are the people with willing hearts.

What do people say is impossible? That is where great opportunity is hiding. If you have a heart that believes and is willing, what great thing could you do?

"Believe in yourself. You gain strength, courage, and confidence by every experience in which you stop to look fear in the face...you must do that which you think you cannot do." –Eleanor Roosevelt

There are things that all of us are afraid of. For some people it is the fear of failing. We know by now that failure is not something to fear, but to learn from. Other people are afraid of people and what they think about them. They let someone else's opinion be their opinion of themselves. That gives other people a lot of power over you. Some are afraid that someone might say *no* to them. Some are afraid to talk to people because they think the other person looks down on them. We all are afraid of something.

If you want to succeed in life you are going to have to train yourself to look at fear in the face and say, "You cannot stop me!" You must be able to do the things that scare you. When you do, you will have more confidence in yourself. You will feel stronger, because you beat the fear that time. It doesn't mean that you don't still get scared of doing it, but you have done it once, and it gets easier the next time.

I used to be afraid of talking to people that I had just met. I didn't know what to say to them. I felt inferior, or not as good as them. Remember that I had believed negative messages about myself for years and years. I felt like a loser. I felt that everyone was better than I was. I had no confidence in myself. Guess what? That chance to make some extra money that my friend told me about REQUIRED me to talk to people. I had to talk to people that I knew and to meet new people and talk to them. I mean there was NO way for me to make any money unless I talked to people.

What did I do? I watched my friend for a few weeks. I studied how he talked to new people. Then I had to go out and do it myself. I started with one. I met someone and talked a little. It wasn't a huge thing, but I did it! The next time was a little easier, and I could talk more. It kept getting easier each time. The other day I was meeting with someone and telling him about how far I had come. He said that he never would have known that I had trouble talking to people I had just met! That made me feel good. It shows me that I have grown past this fear. That is just one example.

So what happens when you do something you are afraid of? You feel better about yourself. You gain strength. You believe in yourself. You get the feeling that you can do anything because you know that you are stronger than your fear. Someone said it this way, "A critical, fundamental step toward any achievement is to tell yourself you can do it. It's simple. It's positive. And it works. Put the power of your own belief to work for you. Tell yourself you can." You must remember that it takes more than just saying that you can. You must take action with that belief and DO IT!

Where does a 600 pound gorilla sit? Anywhere he wants

to. You must do the things that you think you can't do. When you do them, you come out of it as the 600 pound gorilla. You can start doing whatever you want!

Chapter 7

Perseverance

Never give up! That's what perseverance means. It is the attitude that nothing will stop you. I don't know what else to say about it. Never quit. Don't give up. If at first you don't succeed, try again. The only way to fail is to quit. Winston Churchill said, "Never, never, never, never give up." Do you get what I'm trying to say?

❧

"The race goes not always to the swift...but to those who keep on running."

It seems that Samuel P. Langley and the Wright brothers are turning out to be great examples once again. Samuel Langley was the one with all of the qualifications to make the first flight in a plane with an engine. The U.S. government was giving him money to do his research.

He had his plane ready to fly. His assistant got in the cockpit and the plane was launched straight into the Potomac River. The people and newspaper reporters laughed at him. He got the plane out. Over the next two months he repaired it and tried again. The same thing happened and he gave up in shame.

The Wright Brothers did not succeed the first two times they tried either. They kept running. They didn't have the money from the government. They didn't have as many reporters watching them. After all, they were only uneducated bicycle repairmen. No one expected them to succeed. There were only five people there to witness their triumph! They showed that never giving up pays off. They were the ones who succeeded.

Another thing to learn from this story is that the world will laugh at your mistakes. If you are out trying to do something new and different, the world will watch and tell you how silly it was to even try. If you do succeed, don't expect them to applaud you. Most of them will say that you were just lucky. Michael Levine says, "successful people are very lucky. Just ask any failure." Failures will call your success luck.

"The Tortoise and the Hare" has the same lesson at the end. The hare was fast and expected to win. The tortoise was slow. He just kept going at a steady pace. The hare sped ahead and stopped to rest. He fell asleep. The tortoise kept a steady pace and won. "Slow and steady wins the race."

Make up your mind to never give up. If you fail, keep going. If people make fun of you for trying, remember that one of you will be right in five years. Make sure that it is you and not them. If you succeed, be ready for them to say that you were just lucky. Don't worry about it. You will know that you succeeded through hard work, and the rewards will be yours, not theirs.

"In the confrontation between the stream and the rock, the stream always wins...not through strength but through persistence."

Have you ever been at a beach and looked for rocks in the sand? Have you noticed their texture? They usually aren't jagged or pointy. Most rocks you find at the beach or in a stream bed are smooth and rounded. How did they get that way? It is a process called weathering. Over long periods of time the jagged edges get worn off by the constant running of the water and banging of sand and other rocks against it. It is a great picture of perseverance.

Trying new things is difficult. Your first tries will have some rough edges, mistakes that you make along the way. As you keep going you will get those rough edges knocked off.

You learn from the mistakes. You get smoother. Only through perseverance will you get better. Emerson said, "That which we persist (keep doing over and over) in doing becomes easier – not that the nature of the task has changed, but our ability to do has increased." In other words, if you practice you will get better.

It is hard to persevere sometimes, especially if you are trying to do something differently than the way others do it. In a book called *Rhinoceros Success,* Scott Alexander says that people are either rhinos or cows. The rhinos charge for the things they want. They get up and go for their dreams and goals. The cows sit around and chew their cud. They do things the same old way. They never try anything new. They always make fun of the rhinos because they do too much and sometimes fail. It's hard to fail when you never try anything, so they don't.

When you are being teased for trying and failing, it is easy to want to give up and quit. Don't do it! It is better to fail while trying something and growing than to never fail because you never got out of the pasture. Even if you fail thousands of times, when you succeed it will be a great triumph like Edison's light bulb. Maybe no one expects *you* to succeed. They may think that you don't have what it takes to do it. If you persevere you will succeed like the Wright brothers. It is always better to be in the arena trying and possibly failing, as Theodore Roosevelt said, than be out in the pasture with the poor souls who live in the gray twilight that know only how to criticize others because of their fear of failure.

Be a rhino!

"Great accomplishments are performed not by strength, but by determination."

Following is a great story about perseverance. Endurance is another word for perseverance, and this is a story of great endurance. It was through the determination of Earnest Shackleton that all twenty-seven of the men he led to Antarctica made it out alive.

Ernest Shackleton was an explorer in the early 1900s. He wanted to be the first to go all the way across Antarctica. He planned to land on one side and take dog sled teams across. Another ship would land on the other side and some dog sled teams would go half way across and leave food packets along the way. Then Shackleton's teams would have food as they went across.

The ship that Shackleton took from England to Antarctica was called the *Endurance*. Little did the men know that that is exactly what they would need to survive the adventure they were headed for. The ship set sail from England in August 1914. It headed for South Georgia Island. It was the last human outpost in that part of the world. They left the island for Antarctica on December 5, 1914. They sailed south toward Antarctica for six days before they entered the pack ice. Since it is so cold, the ocean freezes into chunks of ice packed together. This pack ice moves with the currents and wind from storms.

The *Endurance* was a ship made especially to be able to sail through the pack ice. It would push its way through slowly. This time it had trouble. After a few days in the ice they were stuck. They couldn't go forward or backward. They were simply stuck. The ice was so thick and packed around them that when the chunks pushed together it lifted the *Endurance* up a few feet out of the water. They lived on the ship and hunted seals and penguins to have extra food besides the stuff they had on the ship. There was nothing they could do.

So they drifted with the ice. It was cold. The average temperature was below zero. There were a few months when there was no sun because of the Antarctic winter. Some of the men got depressed and wanted to give up. Shackleton made sure that he had men with good attitudes around the men who had bad attitudes. He didn't want the bad attitudes to infect the rest of the men. Shackleton knew that it would take determination to make it through this. Bad attitudes would make the men lose their determination.

After a few months, the ice pushed so hard against the *Endurance* that it started to lean over. The men could no longer live in the ship. They had to live in tents and buildings made from crates and other wood. Then in October 1915, the ice

crushed the ship. Now the men were stranded on a field of ice floating in the Weddell Sea south of South America. No one in the world knew what was happening to them. The other ship had landed and set out the food packets halfway across Antarctica. They didn't know what had happened. There were no radios in those days.

They saved the three life boats from damage. They assumed that they would eventually come to open water and would have to have boats to get to one of the nearby small islands. The largest of the boats weighed over a ton. Shackleton's plan was to start heading toward Paulet Island where there was food left by a previous expedition. It was a trip of almost 350 miles.

On November 21, 1915, the *Endurance* sank beneath the ice. Their ship was totally gone. The march toward Paulet Island was very slow. The ice was not smooth like on a lake or pond. The pressure of the ice chunks pushing against each other sometimes pushed one on top of the other. It was not easy pulling the heavy boats over the jagged surface of the ice. Finally Shackleton decided that they would have to stop. The ice was moving in the direction that they wanted to go. It was easier to just let the ice do the work. So they waited.

These large sheets of ice were possibly six feet thick. But the constant pressure sometimes made them crack and split in two. This happened a few times right through the middle of their camp. They had to quickly get all of the supplies, boats, tents, dogs, and men to the larger piece of ice before the gap grew too big.

Shackleton grew more determined to get everyone out alive. They could finally see land off in the distance—some of the islands they had hoped to reach. There was no way to get to them. They were too far away to walk, and the pack ice still wasn't breaking up. They had been stuck on the ice for nearly sixteen months.

Finally, the ice started to break up. It was time to use the boats. They would head to one of the nearby islands. All the men and supplies were loaded and on April 9, 1916, they set off. They had three boats. Each boat was about twenty-two feet long. They were crowded. It wasn't an easy trip. The winds and the currents changed frequently. They had to keep changing their destination. Suddenly the winds changed again, this time in their favor. Shackleton decided to head for Elephant Island about 120 miles away. They battled storms and high waves to reach it. It took about nine days to get there, but they were finally on land! But that wasn't the end of the adventure.

"Commitment is a line you cross...It's the difference between wishing and doing."

After 497 days of being on boats and ice, Shackleton's party had reached land. They were about 400 miles from the nearest settlement, and no one in the world knew if they were still alive. No one in the world knew anything about what had happened to them. They had to get to a settlement and get help. On April 20, 1916, Shackleton announced that he and five others would take another boat trip to South Georgia Island, where they had left from in 1914. It was over 800 miles away.

On April 24, 1916, Shackleton and five crew members left on an 850 mile trip over some of the roughest seas in the world in a twenty-two foot boat. It was their only hope of survival. Shackleton was committed to getting his men out alive. He has to cross a line of wishing things were different and doing something to make things different. Too many of us want things to be different but do things the same way. One definition of crazy is to keep doing the same things and expect different results. I've heard it said, "If you want to change some things in your life, you have to change some things in your life."

They faced storms, huge waves, thirst, hunger, and sleeplessness to make this trip. They were at sea for seventeen days! They finally landed on South Georgia Island 522 days after they had left. But the adventure was still not over. They couldn't get around to the harbor. They had to land on the opposite side of the island and walk. They climbed mountains and crossed glaciers and rivers. At one point, they had tried to get over a mountain all day. They had climbed it three times. Each time they got up, they couldn't find a way down. The third time they knew that there was no choice. The had to cross the line again and commit. They slid down the mountain. If they made it, they were almost there. If they didn't, they would die a few short miles from their goal.

They reached the harbor village. As they walked into town they realized that they looked pretty shabby. They hadn't shaved or had hair cuts for over a year. Their skin was black from burning seal fat as a fuel for the cooking stoves (no trees on the ice). The people didn't recognize the strangers. Eventually someone asked who they were. Shackleton stepped forward and replied, "My name is Shackleton." The people couldn't believe it. Everyone had thought that the *Endurance* had sunk in the Weddell Sea. It did, but the men were all safe.

Because of the pack ice around Elephant Island it took several months for Shackleton to get a rescue boat close enough to get the other twenty-two men out. When he got there he found that all were still alive!

The only way those men survived was through great perseverance. They had to fight to live for almost twenty-two months in the worst place on earth. They never gave up! Their ship was called *Endurance,* but the men lived the true meaning of endurance.

Someone has said, "The one who wins may have been counted out several times, but he didn't hear the referee." If one of the boxers in a boxing match gets knocked down the referee counts to ten. If the boxer can't get up, the other boxer wins. This is saying that the one who wins may have been counted out by the referee, but they just got up and kept fighting. They never gave up until they knocked the other guy down and he couldn't get up. You can't win like that in real boxing matches, but you can win like that in real life.

Shackleton and his men were counted out several times, but they always got up and kept fighting until they won. They give us an incredible example to follow.

Chapter 8

Excellence

You can do something just well enough to get by, or you can do it to the best of your ability. You can be mediocre or excellent. People will judge you by the job you do. I know people who have great ability, but they don't do their work with excellence. Their ability means nothing because they don't produce. I know that person well. That person was me.

Excellence is a state of mind. Excellence is in your mind. You can't let others be the judge of your excellence. Their opinions are important. But what you believe about your job is even more important. You are the only one who knows if you did everything possible to complete the job to the best of your ability.

When my students come up and ask if their work is done, I ask them if they think they did it with excellence. They usually have to go back and redo some of it. You are judged on the excellence of your work. Do your work with excellence.

Probably the greatest basketball player ever was Michael Jordan. He came to the game of basketball and raised the standard of excellence. His determination to be excellent in everything on the court made the other players have to step up or get out. You be the next Michael Jordan in whatever you do. You make others step up or get out!

❧

"Excellence is never an accident; it is the result

of high intention, sincere effort, intelligent direction, skillful execution, and the vision to see obstacles as opportunities."

Did you know that *Shrek* was written and produced in one day? The movie that was nominated for the best picture of the year took less than 24 hours to complete. Have you seen the excellent movie? Can you believe the incredible excellence was just an accident? A couple of guys sat down at a computer one morning and started to play around. By noon they had the script written and by 8:00 the next morning it was finished!

Of course that isn't true. The excellence that the movie achieved was a long, thought-out process. Excellence is never an accident, and it doesn't come quickly. To achieve excellence you must plan for it. You must think through the details of the task and plan how to tackle them.

Excellence also will take "sincere effort." In other words, it will take hard work. The planning is just one part. You have to plan your work and work your plan. It will probably require perseverance as well. There will be problems along the way. It may get difficult. Things won't always work out as you planned. You must simply keep going strong!

One of the laws of science is that things go from order to disorder when they are left alone. That means that your health will go downhill if you don't do something to maintain it. Even then, we get old and our bodies just stop working. To do something with excellence takes "intelligent direction." Things naturally fall apart, but humans have the ability to create ways to keep things working the right way. If you want to be excellent you will have to use your creativity to keep things working right together. It has been said, "If you refuse to accept anything but the best, you very often get it." That means that if you won't take anything but the best, you often get the best. You get what you look for.

When things don't go as planned, you must see the problem as an opportunity. You learn something and grow because of the obstacle. That is when a good attitude and perseverance take over. That is also where the mediocre people fail. They quit when it gets too tough.

Nothing excellent is ever an accident. This beautiful world we live in was no accident. Another scientific law is that things don't naturally go from disorder to order. The universe couldn't go from a random collection of particles and start forming into planets, cells, and other living things. The excellence we see around us came from high intention, or on purpose, and intelligent direction. That is where we get our ability to create!

Use every opportunity as a chance to demonstrate the excellence that was put into you when you were created!

"Excellence is the result of caring more than others think is wise, risking more than others think is safe, dreaming more than others think is practical, and expecting more than others think is possible."

Some people will give you credit for your excellent work, but others will make fun of you or be mad at you. Not everyone appreciates excellence. Why do some people react this way to excellence? It may be because they look bad when someone else does something well. They are the ones who do just enough to get by. The excellence you show exposes their mediocrity and laziness.

The quote says that excellence is because you care about doing your best more than others think is wise. They wonder why should you care so much about it. They may say things like, "Don't be a perfectionist." They mean that you shouldn't try to do it perfectly. The reason they don't want you to do such a good job is that it really makes their job look sloppy. Don't expect them to be happy about your excellence. Don't worry about what they think anyway. The people who judge your work will see the extra effort you put in.

Excellence will also require risk. When you strive to be excellent, you risk failure. You risk making mistakes in front of people. You risk them making fun of you for trying too hard. Those people always play it safe. They never try to win. They play only not to lose.

In Super Bowl XXXVI the New England Patriots had the ball with less than one minute to play. The St. Louis Rams had just tied the game. New England was the underdog. No one expected them to be leading during the game. They actually led most of the game. At one point they were winning 17-3. The Rams got two touchdowns to tie the game. The announcers were saying that the Patriots should just play safe and let the clock run down. Then they could take their chance in overtime. But New England didn't come to play it safe. They came to win. They knew that excellence required them to risk more than other people thought was safe.

They marched fifty yards down field in less than a minute. With seven seconds left on the clock, the kicker kicked a forty-five-yard field goal to win the game for the Patriots! They achieved excellence because they risked.

Don't let the people who live in the gray twilight, who know neither victory or defeat, tell you that you shouldn't try so hard or care so much. They want you to come back with them into the herd of cows and to stop being a rhino. Don't ever go back! The herd will keep you from continuing on your success journey. The herd wants you to stay in the pasture and chew your cud like them. Charge ahead with excellence, you big rhino!

"Pride is a personal commitment; it is an attitude that separates excellence from mediocrity."

Any job worth doing is worth doing well. You should be proud of the work you do. You must promise yourself that you will do your best in everything. When you do that, you are on your way to doing things with excellence.

People who do a mediocre job do just enough to get by. They don't take the extra time or effort to make their work excellent. Have you seen other people who do that? At school they race through their work to be the first one done. When the teacher grades it, much of it may be wrong. The person just wanted to get it done so they could do something else. When someone does that, they are doing a mediocre job. They don't take pride in their work.

Pride is a feeling of knowing that you did your best. Have you ever done a great job on something? How did you feel about your work? You were probably proud of it. That should be a goal on all of your work. It doesn't matter if it is a project for school or cleaning your room. You have to do the job anyway, so why not do it with excellence?

It has been said, "Only those who aim for excellence achieve it." You hit what you aim for. When you aim for excellence, you very often get it. Doesn't it feel good knowing that there was nothing more you could have done to make this job better? You did everything you could, and you feel proud of the job you've done.

People who strive for excellence in their work do better in the workforce than those who try to just get by. The boss sees the great job that is done, and that person gets moved to bigger and more important jobs in the company. When the boss sees someone who is always late with projects, or the project is done poorly, that person misses the opportunities to get better assignments. I know you are still young, but the habits you are forming now will either help you to succeed later, or they will hold you back. Do everything with excellence!

What if your doctor didn't do her job with excellence? What if she didn't put all her effort into trying to find out what was wrong with you. What about the pilot of an airplane? Do you want him to do his job with excellence? Of course. You want others to do their jobs with excellence, so shouldn't you do yours with excellence too?

Take pride in your work. Others may make fun of you for putting in the extra effort, but that's fine. You have the feeling of knowing that you have done your best job. They only have the feeling of concern that someone will find out that they are lazy! Which feeling would you rather have?

"By failing to prepare you are preparing to fail." **–Benjamin Franklin**

"The man who is prepared has his battle half fought."
–Cervantes

Tiger Woods started playing in the PGA golf tournaments when he was still a teenager. He became the youngest player to ever win the Masters tournament. He came to the PGA and started beating all of the old pros by big scores. How did he do it? He prepared for excellence daily.

Tiger practiced the basics of golf daily. He spent hours on the putting greens, at the driving range, and on the course. He practiced, practiced, and practiced some more. The older players would practice, but not as much as Tiger.

Tiger and his coach knew that you have to prepare for excellence. It isn't an accident. It doesn't just happen. It is planned and practiced for. They also knew that if you fail to prepare or practice, you are setting yourself up to fail. That's what Ben Franklin's quote means.

In the first few years that Tiger was in the PGA, the average scores of all the golfers went down. They got tired of this young punk beating them every week, so they started practicing more. Everyone improved their game because they started to prepare more. Tiger raised the level of excellence, and everyone else either had to step up or get out.

Preparation sets you up to succeed and reach excellence. If you do what you can ahead of time, then you are half way to the goal. Half of the battle to succeed or achieve excellence is reached when you have prepared. That is what Cervantes is saying. Does a general go into battle without knowing how many of the enemy there are? Does the president get up to give a speech without looking at it first? Do you take a test without studying for it?

Prepare as much as you can BEFORE you go into battle, or tests, or a game. The time you put into preparing or practicing will get you ready to reach the excellence you desire. You can be the one that sets the standard of excellence that everyone else is trying to reach.

"Every job is a self-portrait of the person who did it. Autograph your work with excellence!"

How do you look at the tasks that you have to do each day? Do you think they are important or boring? How you look at them is important. If you don't value them then you won't care how they are done. It won't matter to you if they are done well or not. Other people are looking at how you do things.

Everything you do shows others what kind of person you are; it is a picture of you. It reveals your character. It answers questions like: Are you reliable? Do you do what you say you'll do? Is your work done well? Can you be trusted with more responsibility? These are important questions about you that should be answered with a big "yes."

How do you answer these questions for people? Do your absolute best job on everything that you do. I mean everything. People—your parents, teachers, and others—will think highly of you. They will trust you to do important jobs. You will show that you are responsible enough to handle it.

Another benefit is that you will feel good about yourself. When you do your best on a project, it gives you a feeling of pride. I've heard it said, "Don't die wondering." It means that when you have finished anything, don't be left wondering if you could have done something better.

Another important thing to think about is that the habits you are forming now will be part of you as you grow. Kids who do just enough to get by grow up to do the same. They don't go very far in their jobs because their bosses can't trust them with more responsibility. If you do your best now, you will get into the habit of always doing your best. You will do better in your job because the boss will be able to trust you. It may even help *you* to become the boss!

"Don't die wondering!" What a great line to memorize and live by. Whatever you do, do it to the best of your ability. Don't hold back one bit. This habit and attitude that everything you do will be done with excellence will speed you along on the success journey.

"Countless, unseen details are often the only difference between mediocre and magnificent."

Pride in your work will show up in the little details. Some people have tried to forge some of the great paintings. They have tried to paint the picture again and make people think it is the original. The way that they always get caught is when an expert looks at the details. Any good painter can copy one of the masterpieces in any museum. If you looked at the two from a distance they would look identical. But when you look at the fine details, you can tell the two apart.

A Rolls-Royce is a very expensive car. They were hand made in the early days. One day, Henry Rolls was walking through the factory where some of the parts were being made. He heard one of the workers look at a part and say, "Oh, that'll do," as he tossed the part in the bin. Mr. Rolls went to the man and said, "That may do for anyone else, but it will not do for Rolls-Royce." Mr. Rolls took pride in the quality of his cars. He wanted every detail to be perfect. All of the little details of the car were what made them excellent.

You may think that one little detail won't matter, but the little details add up. If each worker in the Rolls-Royce factory said, "Oh, that'll do," then the car would be put together with hundreds of parts that weren't perfect. Then you would end up with a car that doesn't have the quality of excellence. If you looked at the car on the outside, it would look great! But inside, the details that must work properly to make it run wouldn't be right.

During the 1960's America built the Apollo spacecraft to take men to the moon. The Saturn V rocket, Lunar Module (LM), and Command Module(CM) had about a million parts. Like the Rolls-Royce car, if all the pieces weren't made with excellence there could be a problem. And that problem could kill the crew. One of the NASA managers said that if they achieved 99.99% perfection of the million parts, that would still leave over 5,000 parts that could malfunction. One of those faulty parts found its way onto Apollo 13. The explosion it caused almost cost the lives of the three astronauts.

Whatever job you are doing, make sure that you pay attention to the small details. Those details, each done with excellence, multiply the excellence of the final product.

"This is the beginning of a new day. You have been given this day to use as you will. You can waste it or use it for good. **What** you do

today is important because you are exchanging a day of your life for it. When tomorrow comes, this day will be gone forever; in its place is something that you have left behind...let it be something good."

Have you ever seen a picture of those magnificent churches in Europe? They are called cathedrals. Some were built over 800 years ago in the 1200s. There were no big cranes, bulldozers, steam shovels, or other big machines that you see around construction sites now. Everything was done with hand tools and hard work. It took between eighty and ninety years to build.

The guys that laid the bricks and worked with the stones were called masons. In those times there were master craftsmen, apprentices, and laborers. The master craftsmen were the ones that had worked at their craft until they were very skilled. They had apprentices that were learning from the master because they wanted to be a master someday. The laborers were simple workers. They didn't have skills. They just did the heavy lifting and hauling of supplies to the masters and apprentices.

There is an old story about three men working on one of the cathedrals. Someone came by and asked each of them the same question. The man asked the master craftsman what he was doing. The mason replied, "I'm laying bricks." And he went back to putting down mortar and placing another brick in the wall.

The man went to the apprentice and asked him what he was doing. He replied, "I'm hauling bricks for the masters to put in the wall." And he went to the pile to get another load.

Then the man went to the laborer and asked him what he was doing. The laborer was doing the hardest of all the work. He also got paid the least for his work. But he had the best attitude. He replied with respect, "I'm building a cathedral!"

The laborer understood that time is valuable. You will trade a day of your life for whatever you do today. Would you sell your last day to be able to watch TV all day? Would you trade your last day to sit and play video games? Use each day to make a difference. Use each day to do something that will last and be important in the future.

There was an old commercial for a hand-held racing game where the kid crashed and his friend asked him if he was going to retire. The other boy replies, "I'm only eight years old." That may be how you feel now. All this stuff seems so far away in the future. You may be saying, "I'm only ___ years old. Does it really matter what I do today?" I say yes, it does! It matters very much.

Everything you do, good or bad, shapes you (more on that later). Let's look at it in a situation you understand very well.

Each day during the school year, do you go to school, or do you go to learn? And don't be fooled into thinking that they are the same thing. That is the same question as asking do you carry bricks, or do you build a cathedral? What value do you put on the activity you are doing each day? There is a difference between going to school and going to learn. If you see the activity as going to school, then you will not put value on it. You won't get as much out of it. There is an old saying, "You get out of something what you put into it." If you don't value the activity, you are wasting your time. You will be trading a day of your life for nothing of value.

On the other hand, if you go to learn, you will put value on what happens in your classroom. You will put more into the activity, and you will get more value out of it. You will be investing your time in YOUR future. You will trade a day of your life for learning. And learning will grow each day into a more powerful force in your life. You can waste each day or invest each day. How do you see your daily activities?

Chapter 9

Courage

Many people are afraid of basically two things: the fear of failure and the fear of people. We have seen already that failure is not a thing to fear. There are great lessons to be learned from failure. The other thing that people fear is other people. Most people's thoughts about themselves are given to them by other people. Think about it. Are you afraid of some people because they make you feel dumb? Or ugly? Or like a loser? If you are, that person has a lot of control over you. You may fear to do things because you fear what that person would say about you.

Courage is the opposite of fear. Courage lets you step out and try new things because you don't fear failing and you don't fear what other people may think about you. Some people think courage is not being afraid. They think courage is being brave in the face of danger. That is true to a point. Ask most heroes who did something brave in the face of danger, and they will tell you that courage is doing what needs to be done even though you are afraid.

You may be afraid to try something, or afraid of what people might think, but be strong and courageous. Do it anyway—that is true courage.

৵

"Courage is daring to take that first step, or a different path. It is the decision to place your dreams above your fears."

"A journey of a thousand miles begins with a single step," someone has wisely said. You will be afraid of trying things. You may feel fear of what other people will think. It will take courage to take the first step. The first step is just that, the first step. You have to follow the first step with the second step, and the third, and the fourth, and the... you get the picture.

Why shouldn't you be afraid of what other people think about what you are doing? Because you are taking steps to make your dreams come true. You have decided that your dreams are more important than your fears—fear of failing and fear of people.

Courage is also the decision to take a different path. You will face this in the near future if you haven't already. It's called peer pressure. That is when your friends want you to do something that you don't want to do. They may call you "chicken" or "scaredy cat" or worse. It takes courage to take the different path. It takes courage to stand up for what you believe is right.

Winners act on what they believe. You don't let the group decide what is right for you. It may be hard, but you know what is right and you do it. You have character. You know what things are right and wrong. Act on those things. Be courageous.

"Fear is the darkroom where negatives are developed."

A darkroom is where pictures are developed. I used to work in the darkroom in the basement with my dad when I was little. I loved those times. A darkroom is called a darkroom because it is a dark room. The film can't be exposed to light. If it is, all of the pictures on the film will be ruined. The paper that the pictures are put on is also sensitive to light. If light hits the paper, you can't print a picture on it. The paper is ruined.

Film is developed in a darkroom. After the film is developed, it is called negatives. Fear is like a darkroom. It develops the negative feelings and thoughts in you. It makes pictures in your mind that seem real. The pictures come from the negative thoughts, so the pictures are negative pictures. The pictures are pictures of you failing. They are pictures of you too afraid to try something. They are pictures that keep you from trying and succeeding.

"Real difficulties can be overcome; it is the imagined ones that are unconquerable," said Theodore N. Vail. We can beat real enemies. It is the monsters that we imagine in the closet that are hard to beat. Wrong information that looks real (imagined) causes fear. That is the hardest fear to overcome.

How do you keep fear from controlling you? "Just do it!" as the Nike ad says. You will feel fear about things. That doesn't mean you are a coward. It means you are human. But to conquer fear, you have to have courage and decide that your goals and dreams are more powerful than fear.

People have studied how fear controls people. They found that when someone keeps thinking about what they are afraid of, the chances of that thing happening go up. As a person thinks about the bad thing happening, they are actually putting themselves on a path for it to really happen. It is just like when you think about positive things. That puts you on a path that makes the chance of you succeeding go up.

You become what you think about. Don't think about the negative things that could happen. That will cause fear, and you won't do anything to move forward. Choose to think about positive things that you want to do.

Courage does not always roar. Sometimes, it is the quiet voice at the end of the day saying, "I will try again tomorrow."

Have you ever had a tough day? Of course you have. We've all had bad days. You tried your hardest but still failed. Nothing went right for you. Sometimes you feel like quitting. Remember those kinds of days? You don't feel very courageous, do you? The good news is that courage isn't always looking fear in the face and roaring at it. It doesn't mean that you always have to pound your chest like an ape. Courage can also be just saying quietly, "I'll try again tomorrow."

Courage is the attitude of never giving up. You will have days where things don't go your way. There will be tough days.

They are a part of life. Sometimes people lose hope and give up. They think that this is just how life is going to be for them. They become a "timid soul" who never experiences victory because they refuse to compete! They lack courage to fight the negative feelings. Courageous people know that things will get better. Those rough days don't last forever. They look to tomorrow with hope that things will get better. They look at failures as learning experiences. They look at fear and say, "You can't control my life. I am in control, and I choose to go on with a great attitude!"

Have you ever seen a great team lose a game and then come back and just kill the next team they play? They have that courage to say, "We failed today, but there's always tomorrow." They learn from the failure and come out with fire in their bellies for the next game. The Chicago Bulls were a team like that in 1998. They set a record for the most wins, seventy-two, in a season. They only lost ten games that year, but never two in a row. They expected to win, and when they lost they came out to win the next game no matter what!

Learn to go on to tomorrow after today was not so good. Your attitude toward what tomorrow will bring affects what tomorrow brings. If you expect tomorrow to be just another bad day, it will be. If you expect that it must be better than today, it will be. The power to choose gives you the final say!

"A ship in the harbor is safe...but that's not what ships were made for."

Is an eagle born to walk on the ground everywhere it goes? Is a lion born to chase mice in your house? Is a rocket built to stay on the launch pad? Is a ship built to stay in the harbor? The answer to these questions is a big NO! Eagles were born to soar. Lions were born to chase gazelle on the open plains. Rockets were made to leap from the launch pad and thunder into space. Ships were made to ride the waves of the open sea.

Were humans made to live small lives going to and from work five to six times a week, fifty weeks a year, for forty years? No! You were made to soar like the eagle. You were born to chase your dreams like a lion. You have the ability to launch yourself to great heights like the rocket. You were given the equipment to navigate the wide open seas.

There is risk to soaring. Does that stop the eagle from living as it was made? Sometimes the gazelle gets away. Does the lion stop hunting? Rockets have been known to malfunction and explode. Has that stopped rocket launches? Ships sometimes aren't able to stay afloat in the storm-driven waves. Does that stop ships from leaving the harbor and taking on the sea? Of course not!

Rising above other people and making your life soar is risky. Does that stop you from succeeding? Sometimes your dreams get away. Does that keep you from chasing the next one? When you leap for new heights and miss, do you stop leaping? The waves make it hard to navigate the ocean sometimes. Do you return to the safety of the harbor and never leave? Never! You are not afraid of these things. You have courage to feel the fear and go on anyway. Failure can't stop you from soaring. Failure can't stop you from chasing your dreams. Failure won't keep you from leaping to great heights. Failure won't keep you safe in the harbor.

You were made to live a life of adventure. You were made to win. You were born to do great things! You are a majestic eagle. So soar! You are a fierce lion. So hunt down your dreams! You are a mighty rocket. So leap to great heights! You are a sturdy ship. Get out of the harbor!

"Truly successful people have learned to do what does not come naturally. Real success lies in experiencing fear and aversion and acting in spite of it." —Joseph Mancusi

I've said it before, everyone has fear of something. Truly successful people feel fear too. They have learned to do what doesn't come naturally. Most people feel fear and avoid what causes the fear. They stay away from it. Successful people feel fear, but do it anyway.

Last summer was incredible for my son and me. We got to meet a racecar driver. It never would have happened if I didn't conquer my fear. We had seen this driver, Michel Jourdain

Jr., the summer before at a track. He was sitting and eating between practice sessions. My son, Joshua, was three at the time. He was so cute with his little racecar T-shirt that I made for him. He held up a card with the driver on it and a marker. Michel waved us into the tent and signed the card and talked to us. He won a few new fans by doing that. Later in the year we saw him at another track. He let us come where they were working on his car. Then he signed a hat, and I got a picture of him holding Joshua.

I sent an email to the race team telling them how cool he had been. Someone from the team emailed me back saying thanks. She said that she would introduce us to him again if I told her which races we were going to be at. I told her that we had made a model of his car and would like him to autograph it. She said that it wouldn't be a problem.

She set up a time for us to meet him at Detroit. He came out and talked to us. He let Joshua sit in his car. I got a picture of that too. He signed the model for us. That was a very cool day. But it gets better.

I used to be afraid of asking people for special favors. What if they said "no?" I thought that they were rejecting me. I couldn't handle rejection. So I didn't ask. But I was learning that the worst thing they could do was say "no." What's the big deal? So what if they say "no." They could also say "yes!" I wonder how many neat things I have missed because I was afraid to ask.

They were going to be racing in Chicago that summer. I live close to the track, so Joshua and I were going to go all three days. It was also the weekend of Joshua's 5th birthday. I acted even though I was afraid. I asked the lady from the team if they could do something special for Joshua's birthday. She said YES! She had Michel come down to see Joshua. He also gave him a visor from his helmet. He signed it, "To Joshua: Happy fifth birthday. Your friend, Michel Jourdain." Some of the teams sell those autographed visors for $100. He gave Joshua one for his birthday. It was also special because it was a visor from the last race where Michel came in third place! They also had a cake for Joshua. That was a great weekend.

We got to see him one more time that year. He came out special just to see us. He signed all the pictures we had of him and Joshua. He gave a visor to Alyssa, my three-year-old daughter. He gave us his email address so we could keep in touch with him.

But what if I didn't ask? All of that cool stuff would never have happened if I hadn't asked. I can't wait to go to the track this year. All I have to do is email him and tell him we'll be there. We'll be able to see him and hang around.

Learn to do what doesn't come naturally. Face fear and act anyway. Don't run from fear like most people. Stand tall and act. You will overcome your fear and move closer to your dreams! I don't mean do something stupid like swimming toward a great white shark or jumping off a bridge. I mean face your fear of failure and fear of people. Don't be afraid to ask. You'll be amazed at the cool things you get to do if you just ask!

"The size of a person's world is determined by the size of their courage."

This world is a world of endless possibilities. There are things that haven't been invented or discovered yet that will change our lives. The people who invent and discover these things will be people of great courage. As they are working on their invention, as they explore new things, people will say that it can't be done. There has always been, and will always be, people who say it can't be done. Albert Einstein said that people with "Great spirits have always had violent opposition from mediocre minds." That means that people who dream of doing great things with their lives are always made fun of by people who just do what is necessary to get by.

Courage will keep these "great spirits" moving forward with their inventions and exploration. Their courage gives them a larger world to live in. Their world has more possibilities than the poor souls that live in the gray twilight that know neither victory nor defeat that Theodore Roosevelt talked about.

As your courage grows — as you face fear and move forward anyway — the possibilities of your life grow. You will try more things because you have courage to try. You don't fear failure or other people, so you can try. You can do. You can experience more in your life.

Michel Jourdain was replaced at the end of last season. The team got someone else to drive the car. He was out of work if he couldn't find another team to hire him. The problem is that the teams get money to run a car from a sponsor — you know, the name of a company on the side of the car. They pay the team a lot of money to have their name on the car. It is advertising for the company. No team would hire Michel because they didn't have a sponsor for him.

Michel looked at the fear of not having a car to race and went to work anyway. He called companies all over Mexico (where he's from) and asked them to be his sponsor. Most of them said "no." He kept looking until he found one that said "yes." He had the courage to move past his fear. His world got bigger because he did.

He got a sponsor and found a team that would hire him. It happened to be the team that won the most races the previous season. He had a teammate that was the champion a few years ago. This opportunity is the best thing that has happened to

him in his career. He has had great success with this new team. He has improved each race. I was even there to see him win his first race!

While he was looking for a sponsor, I had courage to approach a large company and ask them if they would like the opportunity to sponsor him too. I had less fear because I had asked the lady at Michel's old team about the birthday surprise for Joshua. So, I emailed someone at the company and gave him a few reasons why I thought his company would benefit from sponsoring Michel. He said they couldn't do it this year but to ask him again about next year. My world became bigger because I had the courage to act. Next time it will be even easier because I acted this time. My courage will continue to grow, and so will the world of possibilities open to me.

In Star Wars, Ben Kenobi has Luke Skywalker fight a little flying droid that shoots little stun lasers. Luke looks awkward the first few times and gets shot by the lasers. Then Ben puts a helmet on Luke. The helmet has a face shield so he can't even see. Ben tells him to reach out with his feelings. Luke does and he stops the laser blasts without even seeing them. Ben congratulates him and says, "You've taken your first steps into a larger universe." What are you turning away from because of fear? What action could you take to face the fear? A larger universe awaits you on the other side of action.

Chapter 10

Growth

When a pond or body of water is stagnant, or has no outlet, it slowly starts to die. Have you ever seen a pond with a scummy film on it? There is no way for the water to move out of it. It changes as the oxygen is used up. The animals living in it start to die. It can't support life, because it is trapped where it is and can't renew itself. People are like that too. If they don't grow, they slowly start to die inside. Their dreams and life goals go first. Then they just fight to survive.

Winners don't stay at the same level for very long. They are always learning and growing to the next level. They know that if they stop growing they will start to die inside. They refuse to let that happen. The only way to avoid it is to grow, to renew themselves, so life can thrive in them.

There are different areas in which to grow. You need to grow in each of them constantly. The first is knowledge. You learn more information about whatever you are doing to do it better. Another area is in your attitude. We've already seen how your attitude is your most powerful weapon in beating the grumpies. You need to develop your ability to find the horse in the room of manure. Third, your goals and dreams have to grow. You will get some of the goals. Then you need new ones to replace those. All of the goals you get should lead to your dreams. Your dreams will also grow over time. They will get bigger as you see yourself succeed! Fourth, your character must grow. Character is who you are when no one is looking. Are you honest when no one is around? That is character. You must become more trustworthy, responsible, honest, caring, respectful, and fair.

Winners renew themselves each day. They try to grow a little each day. They let the old bad habits out of the pond and bring in fresh good habits. Winners keep from becoming stagnant so they don't die inside.

"There are no uninteresting things, there are only uninterested people." –G.K. Chesterton

One mark of a winner is that they find value in all things. Kids are the biggest winners! They wonder about everything. Why is the sky blue? Where does the wind come from? How does that work? They are interested in everything. It isn't until they've been told to stop asking so many questions that they stop being interested in things.

The world is an amazing place! It is designed to make you wonder about things. It is made to be interesting. Everything in our world is interesting. One way to grow is to get more knowledge. That means to learn more things about our world and how it works. Growing people are always adding to their learning. They are interested in learning the "whys" and "hows" of the world.

There are many people who don't wonder about things. They aren't interested in learning about "how" and "why". They are just uninterested people. They probably were told too many times to stop asking questions. They have lost the wonder of the world. They no longer grow because there is little that interests them.

Don't let anyone tell you that you ask too many questions. That is the only way to learn! In the story *Stone Fox,* the little boy named Willy is asking the doctor questions while she is examining his grandfather. She tells him not to ask so many questions. Willy remembered back to a time that his teacher had told Grandfather that Willy asked too many questions. Grandfather replied, "How's he gonna learn if he don't ask?" Later, Grandfather told Willy, "If your teacher don't know—you ask me. If I don't know—you ask the library. If the library don't know—then you've really got yourself a good question!" That's the best advice I've heard. Don't let anyone or anything take away your desire to know the "whys" and "hows" of the world! Don't be an uninterested person.

"The greatest miracle is that we need not be tomorrow what we are today. We can improve if we make use of the potential implanted within us by God."

We all have a great ability to learn. Some scientists think that humans use only about 10% of their brains. Others think that we use only about 1% of our brains. The human brain has more memory and computing power than a thousand of the most powerful computers. And we use such a small amount of that power.

There is huge potential within us. Ninety to 99% of our brain doesn't even get used. That's a lot of potential! What things would you like to do? The limits are your own doubts and fears. If your mind can think of it, your mind can do it.

A great thing about our lives is that we don't have to stay where we are today. We have this huge potential in us. We can change. I'm going to tell you something that I want you to remember. It is very important that you remember this. It will be very useful someday. Someday you are going to come across an opportunity to do something new. I don't know what it will be for you, but it will be an important and life-changing opportunity. I'm not saying that you should say "yes" right away. What I'm saying is that you should not be quick to say "no."

Most people get a life-changing opportunity at least once in their lives. Many of them say "no" right away because they look at the skills and abilities that they have NOW and don't think they could succeed at the opportunity. I want you to really look at the opportunity. It may not be for you for many different reasons. The one thing that you should not do is turn down the opportunity because you don't think that you have the skills or abilities.

You have the potential to grow and learn the skills. You can grow into the opportunity. Don't let your present abilities keep you from an opportunity that could change your life. Please remember this. I've seen too many of the people that I love miss a great opportunity because they didn't think that they could succeed based on the skills they had at the time. Don't let this happen to you.

"The man who does not read good books has no advantage over the man who can't read them."
–Mark Twain

The most important thing you can learn in school is to read. If you can read, and by that I mean UNDERSTAND what you read, then you can do anything in this world because you can learn anything in the world. If you struggle with reading then get help. Ask an adult to help you, and YOU put in a lot of effort. Don't quit until you can read and understand what you read. Almost anyone can read. It is a matter of learning the sounds and putting them together. Don't let someone else's judgement of your reading skills become your judgement. I'm telling you that you CAN get better. It may take a lot of work on your part, but it's the most important thing in the world for your success. One last thing about reading—everyone can improve too. If you are a good reader, you can get better. Keep practicing and *thinking* about what you read. Reading is *understanding* what's on the page, not just saying what's on the page.

There is so much wisdom that is written down. There is so much good to fill your mind with. But you have to pick it up. Those books can't help you if you never read them. Even if you can read them you are no better off than someone who can't read them. As a matter of fact, you are worse off. If you have the ability to read them but don't, you are choosing to keep the wisdom from your mind.

I've heard it said that you'll be the same person in five years except for the books you read. Books can change your thinking. When you read a positive book your mind changes. The things in the book can change your thinking and the way you look at things. What I mean by that is that books can change your attitudes and thoughts. When your thoughts change, your behavior and reactions change. Your actions will continue to change and your habits will start to change. When you replace bad habits with good ones, you start to develop more character. Strong character will lead to success and reaching your goals and dreams.

I have seen this happen in my own life. The last few years I have read some great books on leadership, success, failing, listening, and how to get along with people. After I finish a book I work on applying, or using, some of the suggestions in the book. I pick one or two things and do them for a few weeks. Soon I am doing some of them without thinking about it anymore. Then my habits are changing. When that happens, I can move on to something else. It has been incredible how much I've grown in the last few years. What I'm finding out is that just by reading these books I am putting myself ahead of most of the people in the *world*. Few people choose to read books to improve themselves. Since you are reading this, you have shown that you are not like most of the cows in the world. You are showing that you are a big, grunting, charging rhino! Read! Read! Read!

Keep in the habit of reading good books that teach lessons. You will outgrow most of the people around you! This book would be helpful to keep handy and read a section each day. As you grow and can read better, start reading some of the recommended books (appendix A) to continue your improvement. They are the books I've been reading lately that have changed me. They are the books that taught me the wisdom that I've tried to share with you in this one. Make a commitment to read one of them a year. Wait until you are twelve or thirteen to start them. If you read one a year from that time on, you will be so far ahead of your classmates. When you graduate from college and start your career, everyone else will just be starting to read those kinds of books. Most people don't read that quality of book until they are in their careers and trying to become successful. They will be trying to catch up to you.

Success comes from having character. You are starting to develop your character by reading this book. If you continue developing it by reading the other books, you will develop a positive attitude that will launch you to great heights. Those other people will never catch up to you because you will have years of *good* messages filling your mind to help you. They will be trying to erase years of bad messages. They will never reach your level. When they reach where you were, you'll already have grown to a higher level! Start now to grow each day. Read something positive every day. Surround yourself with people who think like you do. If you do that now, you will be unstoppable!

Chapter 11

Character

Character is the real you. There has been a lot of focus in schools and communities about character—the kind of person you are. Most people agree on a few basic traits that makes a person with good character. They are trustworthiness, citizenship, caring, respect, responsibility, and fairness.

It's easy for some people to do the right thing when they are being watched. The real test of character is what you do when no one is watching. Are you still honest when no one is watching? Do you help people when no one is there to say how nice you are? Are you respectful of people when they aren't around? Having good character is a key to success.

Success isn't making a lot of money; it's making a difference in the world. Can you make money while making a difference? Yes you can. But there are plenty of people who made money but didn't make a difference. They used people to make money, but they didn't care for the people.

You can't make a difference in the world if you aren't trustworthy. Why would you even try to make a difference for people if you aren't caring or respectful? You must feel a responsibility to people to want to help them. You must have character to be successful. Character doesn't happen. You must develop it through practice.

"There is a choice you have to make, in everything you do. And you must always keep in mind that the choice you make, makes you."

Everything you do either makes your character stronger or weaker. Let me say it again, EVERYTHING you do either makes your character stronger or weaker. It is very important to watch the choices you make.

It is also very important to watch the thoughts that you have. (That is the whole purpose of this book, isn't it?) James Allen said, "A man is literally what he thinks, his character being the complete sum of all his thought." He is saying that the thoughts you have are what kind of person you are. The Bible says, "...out of the overflow of the heart the mouth speaks. The good man brings good out of the good stored up in him, and the evil man brings evil out of the evil stored up in him." (Matthew 12:34-35) What comes out of you is what is in you. That's why you have to watch what goes into your mind. What goes in is what will come out eventually.

The little decisions to do what is right that you make every day are important. They are actually more important than the big decisions. The little decisions to do right prepare you to make the correct big decisions to do right. If you are truthful in little matters, you will be truthful when it really matters. If someone can trust you to do what you said in little things, they will trust you when it really means something. By making the correct little decisions you form the habit and it is so much easier when it really matters.

If you make the wrong decisions in the small things, you simply will not be able to make the right decision when it matters most. It's like trying to boil a frog. Let me explain. Humans are warm-blooded. Our body temperature stays the same no matter what the outside temperature is. Frogs are cold-blooded animals. That means that their body temperature goes up and down with the outside temperature. If you put a frog in a pan of hot water it will jump out immediately. You can't boil a frog that way. If you put a frog in a pan of room temperature water it will stay. If you slowly raise the temperature of the water, the frog's body temperature will also rise. It won't notice that the temperature is going up. Eventually, the frog's blood will start to boil and the frog will die.

You are like the frog. If you make the wrong decisions in the small things, you won't notice that the heat is building. When it comes time for a big decision you won't be able to stand the heat. You will boil alive. Your character won't be strong enough to do the right thing.

Make the right decisions in the small things. It's like a picture in a magazine or book. When you look at a picture in a magazine or book with a magnifying glass you see that it is made up of thousands and thousands of little dots of color. Each dot on its own is nothing. You can't see the picture by looking at the single dots. When all the dots are blended together the picture appears. Your little decisions may seem like nothing by themselves. But when you blend all the decisions it shows your character. Make the picture that others see a beautiful masterpiece!

It all starts with your thoughts. Someone said, "Watch your thoughts, for they become words. Choose your words, for they become actions. Understand your actions, for they become habits. Study your habits, for they will become your character. Develop your character, for it becomes your destiny." One thing leads to another. The path of your decisions leads to your character, and your character becomes your future. Promise yourself that you will seek to fill your mind with good thoughts. Your future depends on what you put into your mind!

"We must adjust to an ever-changing road, while holding onto our unchanging principles."

"In matters of style, swim with the current…In matters of principle, stand like a rock." –Thomas Jefferson

These two quotes say basically the same thing. The method, or way to do things, has changed over the years. For example, the way you add, subtract, multiply, and divide numbers has changed from the time of your grandparents. What hasn't changed are the principles of addition, subtraction, multiplication, and division. Have you ever asked for help on your math homework and your mom or dad show you how to do it differently from how your teacher showed you? The style of doing it may be different, but the answer is the same. That is what the quotes are talking about.

There are many ways to do some things, but the answer is the same. Life is ruled by principles that don't change. A principle is a law of life that doesn't change no matter who you are. It is true for everyone. It doesn't matter if you are male or female, black or white, educated or uneducated, rich or poor. A principle is true for all! For example, one of the basic principles of life is called the "Law of the Harvest." The Bible says, "...a man reaps what he sows." (Galatians 6:7) It is also called the "Law of the Farm."

Farmers plow the soil and then plant seeds. That is also called sowing seeds. After the plants grow, the farmers harvest, or reap, the fruit or grains that have grown. The "Law of the Harvest" says that you will get a harvest of whatever seeds you plant. If you plant corn seeds in the spring, you will reap corn in the fall. If you plant wheat, you get wheat. If you plant oats, you get oats.

There are many ways to plow and plant seeds. You can use an old plow behind an ox and do one row at a time. You can use a modern tractor and do several rows at a time. There are many ways to water the plants through the summer. Some people used to do rain dances to please the gods to make it rain. Other people used ditches to get water to the crops. Most farmers use huge sprinklers to do it today. You can try any of the methods. There are many ways to harvest the crops too. You can pick them by hand. You can use a machine to do it. The methods are always changing. What doesn't change is the fact that if you planted corn you will get corn.

Another part of this principle is that you have to plant the seed at a certain time of year. The plants take the same amount of time to grow before you can harvest each year. The plants need a certain temperature range to grow properly. If it takes four months for the plants to grow before the harvest, you better plant them at the right time when the temperature and weather are right for them to grow. The "Law of the Farm" says that if you wait too long to plant, the plants may not have long enough to grow in the right kind of weather to get a good harvest.

What does this mean for you? You aren't a farmer. The "Law of the Harvest" is a principle that works in almost every area of life. The small decisions that you make each day will determine the big decisions that you make. What you sow is what you reap. You can't sow bad decisions and expect a good decision when it really matters. Just like a farmer can't plant weed seeds and expect to get wheat when it matters at the harvest.

You can't goof around in class and wait for the last day before a test to study the material and expect to get a good grade. Some people can do it and get a decent grade. But they didn't get an education. I mean that they didn't really learn anything. They are sowing a habit of laziness. They can't expect to reap a harvest of success in the future.

You can't fill your mind with junk and expect good character to come out. Promise yourself again that you will seek good things to fill your mind. Then keep your promise! If you sow broken promises to yourself, you will reap not trusting yourself. If you sow keeping promises to yourself, you will reap trust in yourself. The "Law of the Harvest" proves to be true over and over again in life. It doesn't matter if you are male or female, black or white, educated or uneducated, rich or poor. A principle is true for all!

"Keep your head and your heart in the right direction, and you'll never have to worry about your feet."

Fill your mind with positive messages. Read books about success, attitude, being a winner, and leadership. Listen to tapes by people talking about these things. Tell yourself that you are a winner every day. Learn from every mistake that you make. Learn new things each day. Fill your heart with love for yourself and others. Find out about the truth of God and His love for you. Then go to try and do something that goes against the things that you know and believe. You can't do it.

The quote is talking about that. If you keep your head and heart filled with good things, you won't have to worry about doing the right things. The right things will be a part of you. Your character will be full of the right things. You will naturally do the right things.

I said in the introduction that I had heard and believed the negative messages that others said about me. Those things *became* me. They said I was a loser. I was a loser. They said that I was ugly. I was ugly. I did things that proved I was a loser and ugly. My actions came from the thoughts in my head and the beliefs about myself in my heart. That was the way that my feet naturally went. Then I changed the things I put into my mind. The things that I believed about myself started to change. Soon the things that I did started to change. It is a slow change. Each day I have to make the right choices. I'm still growing and learning a little each day. That helps me make the right choices.

Get a dog to meow. Convince a cat to bark. You can't do it because it is against their nature. Get a person who is honest to steal. Convince a truthful person to tell a lie. You can't do it because it is against their nature. How did it become their nature? The small choices to be honest or truthful over a period of time formed them into honest and truthful people. What are you filling your mind with? That is where your feet will be headed. If you don't like where your feet are going, change the direction of your head and heart.

"It's not what lies behind, and it's not what lies in front that is important; it's what lies within."

You can't blame your past for today's problems. I heard that about 30%, or 30 out of every 100 people, blame where they are today on someone else. They refuse to take responsibility for their situation.

The future is out there in front of you. You can plan. You can set goals and have dreams to reach for. You can do everything in your power to make the future that you want. But you aren't in control.

All that you have control over is this moment. Oops! It's gone. Now you have this moment. There it goes. At least you are spending them wisely right now by reading this and improving yourself. What's important is what's in you. What's important is your character. That helps you to make the most of the moment that you have right now.

How are you at being responsible? Do you do what you are supposed to do? Do you do your best at what you do? Do you work hard? Do you think about how your actions affect others? Do you accept the consequences of your bad choices? Do you blame others for what happens to you? Responsibility. That's what's important. Is responsibility in you?

Are you trustworthy? Do you take things that aren't yours when no one is around? Can people believe what you say? Do you tell the truth? Can people trust you with their things? If you say you'll do something, can people trust that you'll do it? Can people tell you secrets and trust that you won't tell others? Can people trust you to keep your promises? Do you do what's right even if it is the hard thing to do? Trustworthiness. That's what's important. Is trustworthiness in you?

Are you a good citizen? Do you help make your home, school, neighborhood, or community a better place? Do you get along with others? Do you cooperate with others? Do you accept that others may have different opinions than yours? Do you know the history of your county? Citizenship. That's what's important. Is citizenship in you?

How are you at caring about others? Do you help people in need? What if they can't do anything in return for you? Do you tease kids who are different? Do you feel bad if you see someone else sad? Caring. That's what's important. Is caring in you?

How respectful are you? Do you answer your parents and other adults respectfully? Do you do what your parents ask you to without talking back? Do you let other people have an opinion? Do you treat everyone the way you want to be treated? Respect. That's what's important. Is respect in you?

How fair are you? Do you treat everyone equally? Do you share? Do you stand up for someone who is being picked on? Do you let everyone play? Do you let others go first? Fairness. That's what's important. Is fairness in you?

Those are six qualities that most people would say that someone with good character has. How are you doing on them? Character. That's what's important. Is character in you?

"Tell me what company thou keepest, and I'll tell thee what thou art." –Cervantes

You will become like your friends. Have your parents ever told you not to play with someone in the neighborhood? The reason they tell you that is because they know that we become like the people we hang around with. They see that that child lacks some of the character traits that they want you to develop.

The quote is saying that I can tell what kind of person you are by looking at your friends. Why is that? Why do we become like our friends? The answer is peer pressure. Peers are people that are about your same age. Your friends are your peers. Have you ever been with a group of kids that were doing something that you knew was wrong? Did you do it too? Did you tell them that it was wrong and that they shouldn't do it? Probably not, if you are honest about it. You wanted to fit in. You didn't want to be different. What you felt was the pressure to fit in. That is peer pressure. If you don't stand up for what you know is right enough times you start to change. That is how you become like your friends.

The Bible says the same thing. "As iron sharpens iron, so one man sharpen another." (Proverbs 27:17) It is using an illustration of sharpening a knife. Just like iron can be used to sharpen iron, one man can make another sharper. The opposite is also true. One man can dull another man. The same is true for boys and girls and women. When it says "man" it means a person. Who you choose to hang around is important to your development.

Jacques Delille said, "Fate chooses your relations, but you must choose your friends." You can't choose your family. You can choose your friends. Who you choose as friends is important to what you will become. I started to hang around with people who had hope for the future. They knew how to fail correctly. They were on a journey of success. They tried to grow and learn each day. Guess what I started doing? I had hope for my future. I learned to fail correctly. I started on a success journey. I am growing and learning each day. It all started with choosing the right friends. Choose carefully!

Chapter 12

Now What?

This is your first step to living a life of success. Success is a journey that you take through your life. You build yourself to be successful with each thought, action, and habit. The choices you make, the attitudes you have, and the way you react build you up or tear you down.

Failure is not a bad thing. It can be a great learning experience. It teaches you what isn't working so you can try something different the next time. Successful people choose not to let failure bring them down.

Read this book again. Do it once a year, at least. To get the most out of it, read a section over and over for a month. As you read it, try to use what you are reading. If you are reading about failure, look at every failure and learn the lesson from it. When you read about goals and dreams, write down some of your goals. Set some that you can accomplish in the next week and month. By applying what you are learning, you will form new habits and thinking that will take you forward on your success journey!

Remember that your brain is a very powerful computer. The information that you put into it will affect what comes out of it. Make sure that the messages you put in are positive. The positive messages will fight the negative messages that come at you from every direction. Whenever you hear that little voice in your head telling you something bad about you, tell it to shut up! Start thinking about positive things that you have learned.

Start telling yourself that you are a winner! You are learning to move forward! You have a great attitude! You can do it!

Hang around people who will build you up. Choose your friends carefully. Make sure they are people that think like you do. It may be hard to find kids like that at your age, so you be the leader! Tell them what you know. Let them read your book. Tell them how it has helped you! They will think it's cool and want to join you on a success journey. People like to follow others who know where they are going. You will be a leader. You will be the one to help others be the best they can be.

Keep reading good things. It's the best way to keep feeding your brain. Leaders are readers. As you get older, get tapes or CDs of motivational speakers and books on tape. Use the time in your car as a classroom. You can listen to great books, learn another language, and keep yourself positive during the time in your car. It's all about keeping good stuff going in your brain.

I wish I could know everyone reading this. I wish I could see the great things that you will do with your life. I'll just imagine that every great leader that I see is one of you. I hope that you have gained as much from reading this as I have from writing it. It has changed me. It will continue to change me. I hope that it becomes a part of you too. Reading this is your first step to living a life of success. Don't let it be your last!

Keep charging, you big rhino!

Tell me what you think. E-mail me at
success4kids@ameritech.net

Appendix A

For further reading

Andrews, Andy
Never Give Up and Go For It! Letters from American Heroes; Dalmatian Press; 2002
Never Give Up and Go For It! Letters from Sports Heroes; Dalmatian Press; 2002
Never Give Up and Go For It! Letters from Inspirational Heroes; Dalmatian Press; 2002
Never Give Up and Go For It! Letters from Celebrity Heroes; Dalmatian Press; 2002
The Traveler's Gift; Thomas Nelson; 2002
Alexander, Scott
Rhinoceros Success; Rhinos Press; 1980
Lansing, Albert
Endurance: Shackleton's Incredible Voyage; Carroll & Graf; 2nd edition; 1999
Maxwell, John
Failing Forward; Thomas Nelson; 2000
The Success Journey; Thomas Nelson; 1997
The Winning Attitude; Thomas Nelson; 1996
Mandino, Og
The Greatest Salesman in the World Part 1 and 2; Bantam Books; Reissue edition; 1983
The Choice; Bantam Books; Reissue edition; 1986
Covey, Stephen

Seven Habits of Highly Effective People; Simon & Schuster; 1st edition; 1990

First Things First; Fireside; Reprint edition; 1996

Covey, Sean

Seven Habits of Highly Effective Teens; Bt Bound; 2001

Waitley, Denis

Seeds of Greatness; Pocket Books; Reissue edition; 1988

Carnegie, Dale

How to Win Friends and Influence People; Pocket Books; Reissue edition; 1990

Holtz, Lou

Winning Everyday; HarperBusiness; 1999

A Teen's Game Plan for Life; Sorin Books; 2002

Hershiser, Orel

Between the Lines; Warner Books; 2001

Stovall, Jim

The Ultimate Gift; Executive Books; 2001

Clemmer, Jim

Growing the Distance: Timeless Principles for Personal, Career, and Family Success; Clemmer Group Press; 1999

Made in the USA